THE END OF OUR TIME

NICOLAS BERDYAEV

The End of Our Time

together with an essay on

The General Line of Soviet Philosophy

Foreword *Boris Jakim*
Translator *Donald Attwater*

San Rafael CA

First Edition, Sheed and Ward, New York, 1933
Second, enlarged edition, Semantron Press 2009
Semantron is an imprint of Sophia Perennis LLC

For information, address:
Semantron Press, P.O. Box 151011
San Rafael, CA 94915
semantronpress.com

Library of Congress Cataloging-in-Publication Data

Berdiaev, Nikolai, 1874–1948.
[Novoe srednevekove. English]
The end of our time: together with an essay on the general line of Soviet philosophy/Nicolas Berdyaev.—2nd, enl. ed.

p. cm.
"First edition, Sheed and Ward, New York, 1933"—T.p. verso.
"The title of the original Russian version (published in 1924) is Novoe srednevekovie, The new Middle Ages"—Foreword.
ISBN 978 1 59731 265 3 (pbk: alk. paper)
1. Civilization, Modern—20th century. 2. Soviet Union—Civilization.
3. Europe—Civilization—20th century. I. Title.
CB425.B42 2009
947—dc22 2009022955

Cover photograph by Dorlys Pari

CONTENTS

FOREWORD

This book[1] is the philosophical fruit of Nikolai[2] Berdyaev's first-hand experience of, and reflections on, the crisis of European civilization in the aftermath of the Great War and the Russian Revolution. For Berdyaev this crisis signified the end of modern history, and thus of the Renaissance; and the end of the Renaissance signifies the end of its spiritual basis—the end of Humanism: "That Humanism has not strengthened man but weakened him is the paradoxical denouement of modern history. In the very act of asserting himself, man has lost himself. European man strode into modern history full of confidence in himself and his creative powers; today he leaves it to pass into an unknown epoch, discouraged, his faith in shreds (that faith which he had in his own powers and the strength of his own skill), and threatened with the loss for ever of the core of his personality" (p. 15, present volume). The Renaissance began with the affirmation of man's creative individuality; it ended with the denial of this individuality. Man without God is no longer man: that, for Berdyaev, is the religious meaning of the internal dialectic of modern history: inwardly divided and drained of his spiritual strength, man becomes the slave of base and inhuman influences; his soul is darkened and alien spirits take possession of him.

Berdyaev tells us that the modern age, with its failed Humanism, is being replaced by a new epoch: "the new middle ages," an epoch of darkness, an epoch of the universal night of

1. The title of the original Russian version (published in 1924) is *Novoe Srednevekovie, The New Middle Ages*.

2. "Nikolai" is the more correct form of Berdyaev's first name. The original translations of Berdyaev's works into English used "Nicolas"; in order to avoid confusion this spelling is retained on the cover and title page.

history. Berdyaev asserts that this night is a good thing: in this darkness, which is a return to the mysterious life of the spirit, the destruction inflicted by the previous period of "light" will be healed: "Night is not less wonderful than day; it is equally the work of God; it is lit by the splendor of the stars and it reveals to us things that the day does not know. Night is closer than day to the mystery of all beginning" (pp. 70–71, present volume).

What will the new middle ages look like? Berdyaev reiterates: it will be the end of Humanism, of individualism, of formal liberalism, and the beginning of a new religious communality in which many things that were concealed in the "underground" of modern history will be revealed. The new middle ages will signify "the passage from the formalism of modern history, which has chosen nothing, neither God nor devil, towards discovering the object of life. All the autonomous activities of civilization and social life are reduced to nothingness, the impetus of independent secular creation is spent, and longing is awakened in all spheres of activity for a religious choice, for real existence, for a transfiguration of life" (p. 104, present volume). With the end of modernity and the beginning of the new middle ages, the return to God will begin: "God must again be the center of our whole life—the center of our thought and feeling, our only dream, our only desire, our only hope" (p. 106, present volume).

Faith in the political and social salvation of mankind has been extinguished: the greater part of political and social life has no reality—it is bogus. Over the last few centuries, man's life has moved from its spiritual core, to the periphery, to the exterior. Berdyaev concludes that the world needs a strong reaction against this domination by exterior things; it needs a return to the interior spiritual life, not only for the sake of individuals but for the sake of genuine life itself. "The life of the spirit is either a sublime reality or an illusion; accordingly, we must either look for salvation in it rather than in the fuss of politics, or else dismiss it altogether as false. When it seems that everything is over and finished, when the earth crumbles away under our feet as it is doing today, when there is neither hope nor illusion, when we can see all things in their naked and undeceiving essence, this is the right time for a religious quickening in the world" (pp. 205–206, present volume). This is the new middle ages.

BORIS JAKIM
2009

I. THE END OF THE RENAISSANCE

I

THE academical division of history into three parts, ancient, mediaeval and modern, will soon become obsolete and will be banished from the text books. Contemporary history is being wound up, an unknown era is upon us, and it must be given a name. The old measures of history are no longer serviceable, as we realized with a sudden shock when the World War broke out; the more perceptive minds saw at once that the peaceable bourgeois pre-war way of life would become impossible. The rhythm of history is changing: it is becoming catastrophic.

Those men who had a sense of the future had long been aware of imminent upheavals and had discerned symptoms in the spiritual order beyond the confines of a neatly arranged and tranquil life, for things happen in the reality of the mind before they are made manifest in the external reality of history. There was something shaken and shattered in the soul of modern man before ever his historical values were upset, and the fact that all things are now "in the melting-pot" should not surprise those who have been attentive to spiritual developments.

It would indeed seem that the old, the secular foundations of the West are trembling, things apparently stabilized by use and wont are shifting. Nowhere and in no single matter is solid earth felt underfoot: we are on volcanic ground and any eruption is possible, material or spiritual. The old world, central and western Europe, is suffering itself to be encroached upon by a new: the Far West, America; the Far East, Japan, to us a mysterious almost phantom land, and China. And from the depths of Europe elements are let loose which are undermining the bases of her culture weak with the age of unbroken continuity from a distant past.

He would have been very short-sighted who could during 1914-18 have denied that European civilization was going through a crisis which historically would have world-wide effect and whose consequences would be lost in a far and uncertain future. And it would have been childish and superficial to imagine that external means would suffice to check the vertiginous wave of devastation which came upon our old sinful world and that we could return with a few slight changes to the life of before the war and before the Russian revolution. We are entering into the realm of the unknown and the unlived, and we are entering it joylessly and without much hope. We can no longer believe in the theories of progress which deceived the minds of the nineteenth century and made the near future seem always to be better, more beautiful, and more desirable than what had gone before. We are more inclined to think that better things and finer and more lovable are to be found rather in eternity, and that these were to be found also in the past in so far as the past touched upon eternity and took its rise therefrom.

What is the explanation of this crisis of European civilization, which has long been obvious from many aspects and is to-day reaching its full manifestation? Modern history, now coming to an end, was conceived at the time of the Renaissance. *We are witnessing the end of the Renaissance.*

The heights of culture, the achievements of human creative work both in art and in thought, have long since given hints of the final exhaustion of the Renaissance, of something like the end of a world-epoch. The frantic pursuit of new ways of creation was one proof of it, but what happens in the high places of life has its repercussions lower down. In the very foundation of social life the same end was being prepared. For the Renaissance stood for a complete type of *weltanschauung* and culture and not only for a collection of remarkably fine creations. The life of man, the life of a people, is a whole hierarchical organism in which higher functions are knit inseparably with lower; there is a correspondence between what happens on the peaks of the life of the spirit and movements in the material life of society. So too the end of the Renaissance is the end of a whole era in history—of all contemporary history—and not only the extinction of this or that effective force.

The end of the Renaissance is precisely the end of that Humanism* which was its spiritual basis. Now Humanism was not only the re-birth of antiquity, a new morality and a new movement in the sciences and in the arts, it was also a new view of life and a new relationship with the universe. These things came at the dawn of modern times to govern their history, and now they have come to an end, all their possibilities have been exhausted. The ways of Humanism and of the Renaissance have been fully explored. There is no longer any possibility of advance along them.

In fact the whole of modern history has been an immanent dialectic of self-revelation and then of self-negation of the very principles which caused its first beginnings. The humanist view of life lost its freshness long ago; it has fallen into decrepitude and can no longer rely on itself as it did so movingly in its youth. Destructive contradictions have appeared at its heart, a morbid scepticism has sapped its energy.

Faith in man and the autonomous forces which were his strength is shaken to its foundations. It did once rule over modern history, but modern history is now charged with its dismantling. Man's intel-

* The historical western Renaissance and its Humanism are herein distinguished from renaissance and humanism in general by he use of capital initials.—Tr.

lectual vagrancy, wherein he knew nothing of an authority higher than his own, has not strengthened his belief in himself; on the contrary, it has irremediably weakened it and compromised even that knowledge that he had of his own identity.

That Humanism has not strengthened man but weakened him is the paradoxical *dénouement* of modern history. In the very act of affirming himself, he has lost himself. European man strode into modern history full of confidence in himself and his creative powers, in this dawn all seemed to depend on his own power of making, to which he put neither frontiers nor limits; to-day he leaves it to pass into an unknown epoch, discouraged, his faith in shreds—that faith which he had in his own powers and the strength of his own skill—threatened with the loss for ever of the core of his personality. No, this man born of modern history does not shine; and what a tragic contrast there is between the beginning of his time and the end! Too many hopes have been shattered, and even our mental image of man is clouded. Minds gifted with some power of intuition would readily go back to the middle ages to seek there the real roots of human life—to find man once more. Our time is a time of spiritual decadence, not of ascent. It is not for us to repeat the words of Ulrich von Hutten at the dawn of modern history: "Spirits have awakened. It is good to be alive!" Modern history is an enterprise which has come to grief; it has not glorified man as it led him to hope: the promises of Humanism have not been fulfilled. Man is tired to death and is ready to rest upon any kind of collectivism that may come; and then human individuality will vanish once and for all. Modern man cannot stand up against his own loneliness and his own dereliction.

II

Human powers were unleashed at the Renaissance and through their impetuous play created a new culture and founded a new history. That is to say, the whole culture of this period, which in the schools is called the history of modern times, was the testing of human liberty. The new man, indifferent to divine sanctions, wanted to be the maker and master of life, without help from on high. He tore himself from his religious centre, to which all his life had been directed during the middle ages: he would go forward freely on a free highway. In taking this road it seemed to the modern European that man and the human world had been discovered for the first time, and that in the middle ages both had been repressed; and even now there are still many who, blinded by the humanistic faith, imagine that the discovery of man must be credited to Humanism.

Nevertheless our own time, since it has pushed all the antinomies of life to their limits and has come to a knowledge of its own origins, at last begins to understand that there was a fatal mistake and abuse of itself in the assurance of Humanism and that at the roots of its creed was hidden a virtual self-negation of man and of his fall. When he broke away from the spiritual moorings of his life he tore himself from the deeps and went to the surface, and he has become more and more superficial. When he lost the spiritual centre of Being he lost his own at the same time.

Such turning-aside from the essence of humanity meant the withering of its organic constitution; man ceased to be a spiritual organism, and so false centres were formed at the periphery of his life: the subordinate organs of human life, having lost organic relationship with their true centre, proclaimed themselves to be independent vital centres. That is why man became more and more superficial.

In the present century, the apex of the humanist era, European man stands amid a frightening emptiness. He no longer knows where the key-stone of his life may be found, beneath his feet he feels no depth of solidity. He gives himself up to a surface existence and lives in two dimensions as if he occupied exactly the surface of the earth, ignorant of what is above him and what below. There is then a vast gulf and a formidable contradiction between the beginning of the humanist era and its end.

Right at the beginning the first excited stirrings of liberty were marked by a marvellous, brilliant flowering of works of genius. Had there ever been known in man a creative urge so vigorous as was being shown in those first days of the Renaissance? Thus man affirmed his power to make freely, the liberty of his art. But he was still close to the spiritual wellsprings of life, not yet far on his way towards its surface. Renaissance man is a divided creature, belonging to two worlds, and it is this which makes the complexity and the richness of his creative power. The beginnings of the Renaissance can no longer be taken as merely a reproducing of antiquity, simply a return to paganism. There still remained to them many Christian elements and mediaeval principles, and a man so characteristic of the sixteenth century as Benvenuto Cellini, during the decline of the Renaissance, was not only a pagan but a Christian as well.

No; the Renaissance was not and could not be wholly pagan. Its disciples breathed the atmosphere of the classical past, sought there the source of free creation and borrowed from it the perfect forms of its art, but they were emphatically not possessed by the spirit of antiquity. They were men in whose souls thundered a storm born of the clash between pagan and Christian, ancient and mediaeval, principles. There could be nothing in them of that classic preciseness and that unity which had been lost for centuries, their art could not engender forms absolutely finished and determined, classically perfect. The Christian soul is imbued with the sense of sin, thirsting for the Redemption and reaching out to another world. That is what killed the old pagan world. A renaissance is historically possible if by that word we mean a looking-back at and revival of ancient modes of creation, but by no renaissance can man turn backward and restore an epoch already lived and over. The creative principles of past epochs invoked by a renaissance act in new and very complex surroundings. They come into involved relationships with new principles and produce types of culture quite different from the old ones. Thus the Romantic Movement at the beginning of the nineteenth century could not be a return to the middle ages, for the mediaeval principles to which Romanticism looked had been broken in the soul of man as he passed through his later history. The results which these principles could now bring about would be wholly strange to any form they might have taken in mediaeval times. Friedrich Schlegel may boast of his mediaevalism, but has he anything in common with a man of the middle ages? No more did the men of the Renaissance resemble the men of antiquity, Greeks or Romans. They had lived in the middle ages, they had been baptized, and the waters of Baptism are not wiped away by any return to antiquity, by mingling with them a superficial paganism. Paganism in European Christianity could never be deep;

it could modify the European soul but could never establish its unity within it. The souls of Renaissance men were so complex that they can never have been good pagans. This duality, this complexity, can be studied in the art and life of any key figure of the *quattrocento*, such as Botticelli.

The Renaissance was already alive in the womb of the middle ages and its first stirrings were purely Christian. The mediaeval soul, the Christian soul, became conscious of a will for creation and this awakening takes shape in the twelfth and thirteenth centuries. It is made manifest by a fragrant flowering of holiness, which is the highest point to which the creative spirit of man can reach. It is accompanied by the finest flights of mysticism and scholastic philosophy. The mediaeval renaissance inspires gothic art and the painting of the "Primitives." It is a Christian renaissance. St. Dominic and St. Francis, Joachim of Flora and St. Thomas Aquinas, Dante and Giotto, these show the real renaissance of the human spirit, of human creation, and they have not lost their touch with antiquity. At the time of the mediaeval and Christian renaissance there was already, in the way of making, a relationship with nature, with the thought of man, with art, with the whole of life. The first Italian renaissance, the *trecento*, is the greatest age of European history, its culminating point. The showing-forth of man's creative forces at that time seems almost to be the answer of human revelation to divine revelation. Such was Christian humanism conceived in the spirit of St. Francis and Dante. But the tremendous hopes and prophecies founded on this first Christian renaissance were not to be so quickly realized: many elements in it were ahead of the times. Man had yet to undergo a division of himself, a state of separation; he had to make trial not only of his strength but of his weakness also.

The *quattrocento* is essentially a time of division. It was then that there came the violent collision between Christian and pagan principles, and it had its effects over the whole order of doing and making. In the work of the *quattrocentists* we do not see anything wholly finished. They seem to show more power in intention than in execution, though there is a peculiar charm in this very lack of perfection. It is this division in the soul of the *quattrocentists* that proves the impossibility of a purely pagan renaissance in the Christian world, and their failure was a splendid failure. The forms realized in the works of the succeeding century by the imposing Roman renaissance give the impression of a much greater success, but this perfection of form and this success have no more than the appearance of classicism, there is nothing truly classical about them. Nothing thought of as wholly completed and perfected on this earth is possible in the Christian world. It is not by chance that the art of the sixteenth century shrank rapidly through lifeless academicism into degeneracy; by that time division in man's soul had become in Italy a decadence and a spiritual disintegration. The Renaissance humanists did not break away completely from Christianity, they did not stand out against the Church, but their religious state was one of coldness and indifference. They hoped to discover man by turning deliberately towards this world and away from the other, and that is why they became shallow. The man that they discovered, the man of later history, is forced to wander about on the surface of life, and on that surface, cut off from all communion with the depths, he will have to do what he can with his own effective powers. He will create a lot, but he will end by exhausting himself and by losing the faith that he had put in himself. It was certainly not by chance that individuality in the sixteenth century was found expressing itself in foul crimes. Humanism may have liberated human energies, but it cannot be said that it lifted up man spiritually. It emptied him.

And this consequence was implicit in its principles. There is at the bottom of modern history man's break with the depths of his own soul, between life and its meaning. What point of contact is there between St. Francis and Dante and the sixteenth and seventeenth centuries? The Renaissance has accomplished many great things and brought many precious values to human culture; but it has failed, because the problem that it posed was insoluble.

The first renaissance, Christian, did not succeed any more than did the other, pagan. Now the trend of modern history begins at the Renaissance. In history one can always point out a tragic divergence between theoretical proposals and their practical fulfilment. What has happened in the modern world is wholly different from what was dreamed of by the first humanists and the fathers of the Renaissance. Did they foresee that the consequence of their new view of life, of their break with the spiritual depth and the spiritual sense of the middle ages, of their creative initiative, would be the nineteenth century, with its machines, its materialism and its positivism, its socialism and its anarchism, the exhaustion of the very creative energy that they had let loose? Leonardo, who is considered by some to be the greatest painter of all, is responsible for the mechanization and materialization of our life, for its deadness and for the loss we have suffered of its highest meaning. He did not know himself what he was working towards. There was within the Renaissance all that was needed for its own annihilation. It freed the creative forces of man and gave his powers their highest expression in art, and in that it operated within the realm of truth. But it also separated him from the spiritual fountains of life; it denied the spiritual man, who cannot but be a creator, and affirmed in his place the natural man alone, the slave of necessity. The triumph of the natural man over the spiritual man in modern history had to lead to sterility, to the destruction of Humanism by its own self: the end of the Renaissance.

The Renaissance was an imposing scheme of trying out the powers of man in free play. It was imagined that the whole of life could be a matter of art. Man turned again towards that Nature which in the middle ages he had felt to be tainted with evil, and in her he sought the sources of life and creation. At the beginning of this relation he felt himself come to life again, regenerated. The curse of Nature was removed; the evil spirits which had frightened the people of the middle ages ceased to cause panic. Insensibly to himself man penetrated into the vortex of natural life, but he was not united to Nature interiorly. He was spiritually under the spell of her material beauty, but he did not reach her soul.

The Renaissance had the seeds of death within itself, in its foundations lay the destructive contradiction of Humanism, which on the one hand exalted man and attributed to him unlimited powers, and on the other saw nothing in him but a limited dependent creature, knowing nothing of spiritual freedom. In order to make man greater, Humanism took away his likeness to the divine and subjected him to natural necessity. The Renaissance, based on

Humanism, uncovered the creative powers of man as a natural being, not as a spiritual one; but the natural man alone cannot draw from inexhaustible springs for his creativeness: he drains himself dry, and only the arid surface of life is left. The latest harvest of modern history has demonstrated this, and has brought about finally the self-negation of Humanism, the emptiness of a superficial and unoriented existence, the withering of creative power—the end of the Renaissance. The free play of human forces could not go on indefinitely, and in the nineteenth century it approaches its end. There is no longer a sense of plenty but of nakedness, the difficulties and the worries of life are increased, the fundamental antinomy of Humanism gets worse and worse and becomes its own accuser all along the line of modern history. It makes Humanism become its own opposite. The humanism of Feuerbach and Auguste Comte, apostles of the "religion of humanity," has almost nothing in common with that of the Renaissance; it even undermines the humanist antinomy itself. And it is without any urge of creative forces; rather does it seem to cloak a complete collapse.

The middle ages safeguarded human powers and prepared the way for the splendour of the Renaissance. Man came to this flowering with mediaeval experience, mediaeval preparation, and all that was authentically great in the Renaissance had a bond with the Christian middle ages. To-day man is going towards an unknown future with the experience of modern history and what led to it behind him; he is not full of creative enthusiasm, as at the beginning of the Renaissance, but exhausted, weak, without faith, empty. All that gives us something to think about.

III

It was at its first appearance that Humanism was finest and most fruitful, and all the art that it engendered was of the Renaissance; it might be called "renaissential." At the beginning it had recourse to the everlasting source of human art, to classical antiquity. But it will not do to think that Renaissance art was the fruit of a return to paganism, of a relapse within Christendom: this were to betray a superficial and misguided way of looking at it. Certainly Humanism fed on antiquity, but it was itself a new phenomenon—of modern history, not of ancient.

Man's creative activity was then at its fullest in Catholicism, and the whole of the great European civilization, Latin above all, was grounded on the culture of Catholic Christianity, it had its roots in the Christian religion. This itself was already soaked in antiquity—to what an extent it had taken over the ancient culture is now recognized. That culture still lived in mediaeval Catholicism and by it was carried on into modern times. It was because of this that a renaissance in our history was possible. The Renaissance was not, as the Reformation was, against Catholicism. A tremendous human activity was afoot in the Church, it showed itself in the papal sovereignty, the domination of the world by the Church, the making of a vast mediaeval culture. In this, Catholicism is to be distinguished from Eastern Orthodoxy. Catholicism not only showed men the way to Heaven, it also fostered beauty and splendour upon earth. Therein is its great secret. By seeking first for Heaven and life everlasting there, it adds beauty and power to mortal life on earth. The asceticism of that Catholic world was an excellent training for work; it safeguarded and concentrated man's creative powers. Mediaeval ascesis was a most effective school: it tempered the human spirit superbly, and throughout all modern history European man has lived on what he gained in that schooling. No other way of spirituality could have so tested and trained him. Europe is spending her strength extravagantly, she is exhausted; and she keeps some spiritual life only because of the Christian foundations of her soul. Christianity has gone on living in man in a secularized form, and it is she who has kept him from disintegrating completely.

Humanism in its beginnings was still close to Christianity: it drank at the two springs, antiquity and the Christian religion. It was creative and

eternal significance. The Reformation, on the other hand, was to be more a revolt and a protest than a religious creation, it was to be aimed at religious tradition. German mysticism had been creative, a marvellous manifestation of the spirit, but the Reformation, which was religiously barren, was not its product. At first there was plenty of Catholicism in the Reformation: it was something happening inside Catholicism, Luther was a rebellious Catholic friar, it was Catholic blood that stirred within him. All the really deep and authentically religious elements in the Reformation were bound up with the eternal truth of Christianity; it was a thirst for purification, for renewal, for restoration, in the bosom of the Church herself. Luther had his moment, a single moment only, of high truth: his urgent need of spiritual liberation. Tragically, it was by a negation that he quitted his true path.

The revolt and protest inherent in the Reformation led to the evolution of modern history towards the "Enlightenment" of the eighteenth century, towards Rationalism, the Revolution, and its ultimate effects, Positivism, Socialism, Anarchism. The Enlightenment is but a pale reflection of the Renaissance, a lingering form of humanistic self-affirmation. There is nothing left in this of the creative spirit; the Renaissance has dried up. As for eighteenth-century Rationalism, if it was a phenomenon essentially distinct from the creative spirit proper to the Renaissance it was nevertheless in its genesis related to it. The Enlightenment is the temporal punishment of the Renaissance, the penalty for sins of "renaissential" pride, for that self-affirmation which was traitor to man's divine fountain-head. Thus, in painting, the School of Bologna was the condemnation of Michael Angelo and Raphael, because the spirit that dominated the sixteenth century could bring only death. By such and such ways did the spirit of creation wither. Savonarola was a warning set up against the wrong roads. The Renaissance used up its creative powers in giving rise to a strong historical movement wherein there was to be nothing left of such powers. The French Revolution, Positivism, and nineteenth-century Socialism were at the same time consequences of its humanism and symptoms of its decay.

IV

To reach the Renaissance it was required that the creative powers of man should be gathered in great strength. There was a fine flowering, and this spread over all the course of subsequent history. Man owed this profusion of his to mediaeval asceticism. And yet modern man came to be ungrateful to the spirit that had husbanded his forces. He has lived on an outpouring of creative power; with time that power has become quite spent; and it was left for Europe to-day to dispel completely all the humanist illusions, to come, at a very pinnacle of history, to self-destruction and the shattering of the foundations themselves of human identity.

Everything indicates that man's earthly wayfaring is but a testing time for him, the preparation for another life. All the realizations of ideals in history are so many formidable set-backs. The Renaissance came to nothing, the Reformation came to nothing, the Enlightenment came to nothing; so did the Revolution inspired by the Enlightenment. And thus too will Socialism come to nothing. Throughout all his history man fails to accomplish what he sets out to do. But, unawares, very great values are introduced which he never foresees. The Renaissance fell short of its perfection, the full accomplishment of earthly joy and beauty, and yet its values are tremendous and even its failures are stamped with undying beauty. Witness the *quattrocento*, the very time when man became divided within himself.

The Renaissance was the starting-point of modern times; and the Reformation and the Enlightenment and the French Revolution and Positivism and Socialism and Anarchism are all part of its disintegration, the disclosure of the intrinsic contradictions of Humanism and the progressive impoverishment of the creative powers; and the further we travel from the Renaissance the more do these powers deteriorate. The highest moments are associated with a turning to the middle ages, which direct us back to the main stream of Christianity. This happened, for example, at the beginning of the nineteenth century with the Romantic Movement and at the end of that century with the neo-romantics and symbolists. There is good reason to believe that man's creative forces cannot be regenerated or his identity re-established except by a renewal of religious asceticism. Only such a recall to our spiritual foundations can concentrate our powers and keep our identity from coming to dust. There is nothing else for it now that, at the climax of our later history, the powers of evil threaten again to cast us down. It is no good to yearn for a new kind of renaissance after such a spiritual drying-up and dilapidation, after such wanderings in the desert of life, after so deep a sundering of human identity. By an analogy we might say that we are approaching not a renaissance but the dark beginnings of a middle age, and that we have got to pass through a new civilized barbarism, undergo a new discipline, accept a new religious asceticism before we can see the first light of a new and unimaginable renaissance.

But everything is so used up that we may well ask if human powers may not this time awake turned towards another world. Natural powers have their limits. The natural man's confidence in himself leads to a fall because he has denied the sources of his life: cut off from his spiritual nature, he becomes a prey to illusions and his life is made up of phantasms. It must be recognized that man in his limited and relative earthly life is capable of bringing about the beautiful and the valuable only when he believes in another life, unlimited, absolute, eternal. That is a law of his being. A contact with this mortal life exclusive of any other ends in the wearing-away of effective energy and a self-satisfaction that makes one useless and superficial. Only the spiritual man, striking his roots deep in infinite and eternal life, can be a true creator. But Humanism denied the spiritual man, handed over the eternal to the temporal, and took its stand by the natural man within the limited confines of the earth; and this creature who wanted to rely on himself alone now finds himself defenceless amidst unbridled elements and menacing natural forces. The likeness of man cannot be kept inviolate by the powers of natural man: it postulates spiritual man. The subsistence of human personality is impossible without the life-making stream of religious asceticism, which differentiates, which separates out, which puts first things first. And yet modern history has been built upon the illusion that personality can spread its wings without the help of these ascetic influences.

Modern history, child of the Renaissance, developed individualism, and individualism has been in fact the ruin of human individuality, of personality, and we are witnesses to-day of what comes of an individualism that has no spiritual basis. It emptied man's individuality, took away form and consistency from personality, brought it to dust. It is a general law that human individuality is strong, fruitful, and consistent so long as it recognizes super-individual and superhuman realities and values and submits itself to them. The moment that it denies these things it becomes crippled, withered, good for nothing. Henceforth the motions of the human individual will are aimless, directed towards nothing, and man has been led to this emptiness by a deceptive humanism which has made a wilderness of the human soul. And yet a tremendous problem was raised by Humanism, and the theme of it was man. I see this theme showing itself all through the tragic dialectic of modern history, and the appearance of Humanism cannot be thought of as sheer misfortune, unalloyed evil. That would be a static attitude. The humanist experiment has a positive significance as well. It was in man's destiny that he should live through it. He had to go the way of freedom and freely to accept God. That was the real meaning of Humanism.

V

The phase of Humanism which marks the second half of the nineteenth century and the beginning of the twentieth corresponds to a final extinction of the Renaissance, to the last failure of its powers. The free and vehement play of overflowing human energy is at an end. There is no trace now of the "renaissential" spirit—all that is spiritually significant and effective is by this time veering to the religious and specifically Christian elements in man. The pagan tendencies of our time are superficial and it would be idle to look for any spirit of antiquity in them. The man that stands for this aspect of modern culture is not a man of a renaissance but of a decadence, in itself one of the forms of the dying Renaissance. Man has climbed to the summit of modern times weak and shaken, borne down by the burden of a history made over-complicated by its deviation from its religious axis. Man cannot support the loneliness into which the humanist epoch has cast him; because of it, he breaks up, makes counterfeits of spiritual communion and spiritual ties, forms imitation churches. Materialistic sociological theory is the reverse side of man's inner division and deep isolation, for what is interiorly separate tends exteriorly to unite; in its philosophical sense it is simply the other aspect of extreme individualism, of the "atomizing" of human society. The human individuality which began to assert itself at the Renaissance still lived on organic spiritual concords; it did not show itself as an isolated atom. It had free play and was effective, having a spiritual basis firm beneath it. It was not as yet given over to a socializing process to try and save itself from its own solitude and to escape from its spiritual and material hunger. The making of this process into a religion is the unavoidable *dénouement* of the Renaissance, necessitated by the petering-out of that human individuality which it inspired centuries ago. Extreme individualism and extreme socialism are a choice of evils. In both, man's individuality is compromised and his true likeness darkened, and for the destruction of these abstract Humanism is responsible.

Human identity, like every authentic reality, is only conferred in that spiritual concretion which puts the seal of divine unity on the whole of human multiplicity. In abstraction and isolation it is lost. The process of modern Humanism is the passage from man in this spiritualized concretion, where everything is organically bound together, to a sundering abstraction, wherein man is changed into an isolated unit. Man expected to find freedom, to confirm his individuality, and to acquire creative energy by thus passing from the concrete to the abstract. He wanted to free himself—by shaking off that divine grace which had gone to the making of his own image and which spiritually fed him. Abstract humanism is a breaking-away from and a denial of grace, whereas life is concrete only in grace, outside it is abstract. All the illusions of

Humanism begin here. Whatever seems to man to be emancipation and a recovery of his individuality is only a subjection of his spiritual self to the turmoil of nature, a disintegration of his personality, and this is shown beyond dispute at the apex of the modern historical process. Humanism withdrew man from the concrete, not with all his spiritual affinities and interactions but in an abstract way as if he were an atom contained wholly within himself. This tendency did not show itself in full flower in the early part of the Renaissance, but developed gradually in the course of its later history. It had inevitably to lead to excessive individualism and excessive socialism which are the two forms of the atomizing process, of the abstract decomposition of society and personality. Two men who dominate the thought of the new era, Friedrich Nietzsche and Karl Marx have shown these two forms of self-negation and self-abstraction with the intensity of genius. With Nietzsche it is in its individualist form that Humanism gives way and destroys itself; with Marx it is in its collectivist form. Abstract individualism and abstract collectivism are due to one and the same cause, the withdrawal of man from the divine foundations of his life, his cleavage from the concrete. Nietzsche is the child of modern Humanism and its victim, he suffers for its sins. In his destiny Humanism passes into its opposite. He feels that man is "a shame and a humiliation"; he thirsts to see man overcome himself, he aspires after a superman. Nietzsche's morality does not admit the value of human personality; he discards the human and preaches hardness towards man in the name of the superman, in the name of the future and the distant, in the name of superhumanity. His superman takes the place of the lost God. He cannot and does not want to keep himself human, on the human level. In the superhuman individualism of Nietzsche the image of man perishes.

So too does it perish in the superhuman collectivism of Marx. Spiritually Marx derives from the humanist religion of Feuerbach (in him also, though differently, humanism becomes its own contrary). Marx sees human individuality as a heritage from the old bourgeois world, and he wants it to rise above itself into collectivism. Nor does his morality allow any value to human personality; he also discards the human and preaches hardness towards man—in the name of collectivity, in the name of the future state, the socialist state. His collectivity takes the place of the lost God. He too cannot and does not want to keep himself anywhere on the human level: there is inhumanness and anti-humanity in his collectivism; man's personality vanishes and his identity is lost in darkness. Marxian collectivism does not allow that human individuality of which the infinite interior life was recognized and glorified not so long ago by the humanism of Herder and Goethe. Marx again is a legitimate child of modern history, exactly like Nietzsche. The end of the Renaissance is consummated in both, but in different ways. Nietzsche turns towards the Renaissance and wants to live by its creative impulses, but he moves to a plane from which it is no longer possible to keep contact with it and with the sources of its inspiration. Marx rejects the Renaissance as a thing of the bourgeois world; he covets a new dispensation wherein one may not even dream of plentiful creation. The works neither of Nietzsche nor of Marx show the triumph of man. They have served only to unmask the illusions of Humanism. After them there is no further chance of seeing in it an intoxicating and enchanting ideal, simple faith in man is made an impossibility; and man will be denied once more, by Max Stirner, who will thus deal yet another blow to Humanism. The transitory reign of man, of man sufficient to himself, is going to pieces. The limits and limitations of humanity can be seen, and the boundaries of human possibility have been overstepped: man is not enough. But it is emphatically the Renaissance that is coming to an end, the Renaissance that was a playground for all the forces of man's interim reign. The humanist kingdom promised a life of perfect happiness and beauty, and the humanist kingdom is over. Its growth and extension, its democratization, have killed it: a creative humanism can live only in a small and select society. So it was at the time of the Renaissance. The Enlightenment and the Revolution brought levelling into the humanist paradise, and it worked for its internal corruption. The Renaissance was founded on inequality and was possible only to the extent of the inequality. A passion for equality got hold of man, and the Renaissance was marked for death.

VI

The end of the Renaissance means the dislocation of the organic structure of life which it had retained. The Renaissance, like all organic life, was hierarchical. The movement towards secularization, which was to end in the mechanization of life and the break-up of all constituted organization, was taken in its first phases to be the emancipation of man's effective powers and the exuberance of their free activity. *But human powers that escape from a state of organism inevitably become enslaved to mechanization.* This is not perceived at first. For a time man lives under the illusion that he is independent of all organic ties and he has no suspicion that he will become just a tooth on a wheel in a machine; this intermediate period, which came to a close for Europe in the seventeenth or eighteenth century, was the time of the true renaissance. European society at its highest was watching the activities of human powers already out of touch with their deep sources, but not yet, I repeat, conscious of being controlled by a mechanized uniformity. Then in the eighteenth-nineteenth century there came all of a sudden one of the worst revolutions that has ever swept over mankind: the machine made its triumphal appearance on the stage of human life and promptly upset the whole of its organic rhythm.

Machinery destroyed the age-long pattern and structure of human life as an organic whole with the life of nature. By its check on man's exuberance and by its curtailment of creative increase it killed the Renaissance. It has made a new age, the age of "civilization." Culture and its holy symbolism is dead. The men of the Renaissance did not know and could not guess that they were paving the way for the triumph of the machine in the world, that mechanism would take the place of organism. The organic structure of life is hierarchical, that is, cosmic, and in the cosmic organism the parts submit to the whole and all depend on the centre. The centre is the last end, the object, of the life of the parts. If the parts of an organism break away from the whole and cease to look to their centre they insensibly come under the control of a lower kind of nature.

The men of the Renaissance were proud of themselves because they discovered Nature as well as Man. They desired her abundant blessings, they became learners in her school, they imitated her shapes, and they gave up the struggle which mediaeval man had carried on with her sinfulness; they felt the enchantment of the outward appearances of Nature and the joys of a natural life. Alone certain mystics and theosophists went into these things more deeply. The Renaissance was concerned with a scientific as well as with an artistic discovery of Nature. That was its most significant achievement, for from it sprang the historic triumph of natural science and the colossal technical progress of the nineteenth century that enthroned the machine above human life. So the end of the Renaissance by no means corresponds with its beginnings. The early alliance with Nature, lighthearted and care-free, has been turned into the consciousness of an unavoidable war with her, which we carry on by means of a mechanized life. We do not follow her forms and look for our norms of perfection in them; she is our enemy, because we are interiorly estranged from her and we regard her as a piece of lifeless machinery; our times have set up a Machine between Nature and Man. The relations between modern civilized man and Nature are alone sufficient to show clearly that the Renaissance is over. The immanent dialectic of renaissance relations with Nature leads to a negation of those relations, and the end of the Renaissance kills Nature as it kills Man. That is the tragedy of the new era that we have got to go through. The machine which the Renaissance elaborated has slain the Renaissance and slaughtered the beauty of life begotten by the superabundance of man's creative powers.

The results of the introduction of machinery into man's life are numberless, and they extend to his spiritual life and to all that he does. Science and art are involved in mechanization: they are marked by that break-up of organic unity which the machine entails on everything. Contemporary art, finished with antiquity and the Renaissance, looking only to the future and worshipping the future, is bent on dismembering the human body and its eternal forms; in it the likeness of man must at last disappear.

Futurism,* which is in itself a more serious symptom than one would suppose, does away with the images of nature and of man and with them goes the essential character of renaissance art, which looked only to eternal forms. It throws over the work of Michael Angelo and Leonardo and turns its back on nature and antiquity. For its forms it turns to the machine, for it is caught up in the process which dismembers all unity into mechanicism. Futurists do not see the meaning of the state of affairs in which they are involved, their understanding is inadequate to grasp the significance even of their own movement. Whatever real value it may have, the fact remains that

* Under this term the author would seem to include all such contemporary and pre-contemporary movements as Cubism, Vorticism, Dadaism, Surrealism, Gagaism.—Tr.

both the soul and the body of man perish in such art: they are pounded to matchwood in the inhuman tempest. The Cubism of a great painter like Picasso had already torn man's body limb from limb and overset his artistic identity; futurist painting, wherein the ideas of to-day so soon give place to those of to-morrow, pushes the dispersion of human identity still further: the clarity of natural forms is brutally violated, everything passes into everything else and man into inanimate things; scraps of advertisements, bits of glass, and the sole of a shoe break into some natural form and destroy it. The shapes of the human body are necessarily antique shapes; to destroy them is to break definitively with antiquity.

Similarly does futurist poetry decompose the human soul by mixing it up with fragments of type, glass, and shoe-leather, enslaving it to the noise of motor-cars and aeroplanes. This decomposition was prepared by Impressionism, wherein the soul deliquesced in sensation. Man's centre was gone and, having to look for support within himself, he spoiled his own image. He lost his eternal spiritual bearings and so there he is to-day—a prey to the devastating forces of our time.

Futurism is a product of human self-affirmation and is at the same time a self-negation of humanism. In it man ceases to be aware of his own identity and loses himself in I know not what unhuman masses, dominated by unhuman aggregations. It is not by chance that it has shown itself so well adapted to the extremest forms of social collectivism. The passing of the Renaissance and with it the divine likeness in man may be seen well in the poetry of Andrew Biely, one of the most remarkable of contemporary artists. Biely has a kinship with Futurism, but he goes far beyond the futurists. He transgresses every natural boundary, spoils all the fixed forms of creation; man and the cosmos dissolve in the wildest agitations, human likeness is one with a lamp-shade, a city street, a cosmic infinity. The art of Biely is very characteristic of our age and it is a violation and laying-waste of all the forms of antiquity and the Renaissance: it is something which deliberately sets itself apart from nature, apart from man, apart from God. Contemporary art is more and more involved in this post-Renaissance twilight of man and nature. There is an invasion of barbarous forms, barbarous sounds, barbarous movements; the inner force of this art has lost the inner rhythm of the world.

Positivism was a fruit of the Renaissance spirit but only of its decadence: it knew no creative abundance in the order of knowing; the joyous elation of knowledge eager to unveil the mysteries of nature had vanished. Rather did it witness those mysteries close up again and experience the limitation of man's powers, the weariness that comes from knowledge alone. Pico della Mirandola, a characteristic Renaissance figure, is diametrically opposed to all Positivism; the *pathos* of Leonardo da Vinci is the contrary of Positivism—and yet he had the germs of it in him. In the order of knowing, as in every other, the Renaissance of its nature was bound finally to produce results opposite to those which it intended. The Positivism of Auguste Comte emerged from two opposed principles which ruined the Renaissance spirit from two sides: the rationalism of the Enlightenment and the spiritual reaction away from the French Revolution. Comte was an inverted Catholic, and there were several mediaeval elements in him. He advocated a return to the old principles of hierarchy, organization, authority; he wanted to subordinate knowledge and human life to a spiritual centre again and so put an end to the modern intellectual anarchy. There was good reason why Comte should rate Joseph de Maistre so high—he had got so much from him. But the mediaeval and religious principles of Comtism, perverted forms though they were, did not prevail in the later development of the system: it may even be said that they frightened the positivists. Anyway, the most positivist elements of Positivism were already an anti-Renaissance reaction; it had soon miscarried and ended in the loss of creative principles.

To-day no one can take Positivism seriously any

longer; for a considerable time its high place in European philosophy has been held by Kantian Criticism, which may be regarded as a belated phase of Reformation thought. Contemporary German gnoseology is the latest and most refined spiritual product of the Reformation. As at the sources of that movement there was a revolt of man and an assertion of his rights, so among its intellectual consequences at the close of modern history there is man's desire to, so to say, get rid of himself in the mode of knowing, to get beyond himself, to be above all anthropologism. Contemporary German philosophy, in the persons of Cohen, Husserl, and many others, leads an attack above all in this sense; it is suspicious of man, it sees in him the cause of the relativity and precariousness of knowledge. There is something in Critical Gnoseology which reminds one of Cubism; it decomposes the organism of human knowledge into categories rather as Picasso and others decompose the human body into cubes. By the process of analytical demolition and dismembering of organic integrity Critical Gnoseology breaks up man's image. In it the old spirit of creative superabundance weakens and dies; it again marks the end of the Renaissance. Thus in knowledge itself man reaches self-negation and self-destruction by the way of self-definition and self-affirmation. When he has denied his spiritual centre he has lost himself and lost his eternal image and likeness. He gives himself up to the power of something unhuman. Man can be found sooner in the Scholasticism of the middle ages than in the new scholasticism of gnoseology: it is a product of an era of spiritual decadence.

This same proceeding, the destruction of man by himself in consequence of his trust in his own powers, is to be seen everywhere. To-day Theosophy is at enmity with man and dissolves his image in astral whirlpools; it now no more believes in the reality of his personality than does the grossest and most materialist naturalism. Theosophy is, indeed, only the transplantation of naturalism into the spiritual world. The theosophists of the Renaissance, for example, Paracelsus, held man so high as to submit the problems of creation to him. Steiner and the theosophists of to-day, even though they call themselves anthroposophists, definitely submit man to a cosmic evolution (which nobody understands), and their proposed way of perfection of man by himself is not a creative system. Theosophy denies God; anthroposophy denies man: he is only a fleeting moment of cosmic evolution, he ought to be transcended. Current Theosophy expresses the crushing-down of man, the extinction of his individuality, of his free activities, of his creative powers; he has lost his soul—and must look for it in the flux and reflux of cosmic forces. Theosophical wisdom contemplates the corpse of Nature and the corpse of Man.

All the dominant intellectual life of our time is signed with the sign of the end of the Renaissance. Even the physical sciences have done with it; the stability of the physico-mathematical principles of Newton in face of the universe is disturbed. The discovery of entropy, of radioactivity and the splitting of atoms in matter, finally of the principle of relativity, is like an apocalypse of modern physics.

VII

Socialist tendencies are a characteristic of our times: all our culture and morality as well as our politics and economics are tainted by them; this indicates a real state of mind. Socialism is only the reverse side of individualism, the result of individualist disintegration and severance. It is lying in wait on the passage of society towards "atomization," an internal dialectical fatality: by that road we must come to Socialism inevitably. Socialism and individualism are equally opposed to an organic conception of the world, and Socialism is a glaring symptom of the end of the Renaissance; the free play of man's creativeness ends with it. Human forces are bound to one another and to a common centre: when this centre is no longer religious it becomes social. The principle of collective work, compulsory and organized, takes the place of the principle of creative individuality: man as a person is subordinated to "collectives," to masses. The face of man is hidden by the dark shadow of a collectivism that has no face. Henceforward creativeness will have to yield to standardization. Life's centre of gravity is shifted to the sphere of economics, and the sciences and the arts and all spiritual values are looked on as a "reflex." Man has become an economic category.

Socialism has its origin in humanism and is a direct product of the Humanism of modern times: it would not have been possible without a precedent self-affirmation by man and the transfer of his vital centre to human welfare. But Humanism reaches its own negation in Socialism: the conscience of the proletariat has nothing humanistic about it, it is anti-human. "The class" takes the place of man; the value of his individual soul and destiny is denied, he is simply a means towards social collectivization and its development. Humanism was the father of humanity, in the sense of a moral disposition, and humanity was the reign of the "average man." But this virtue crumbles away under proletarian socialism, for Socialism denounces all its works as delusion. It indicts all the best manifestations of Humanism: its arts and sciences, its morality, the whole of its culture; the humanist structure is pulled down, its foundations laid bare. And these foundations are discovered to be simply economic class-interests. Truly, if man is separated from his true centre and his spiritual origins his life can only have a material basis and a deceptive superstructure; he is lost among "interests" and the integrity of his human nature is broken up into class-organization.

In one sense Marx was right in regard of nineteenth-century bourgeois society. "Humanity," which Herder looked on as the object of history, was decomposing, the underlying economics played the most important part and all culture anticipated the "reflex" rather too much. Economic materialism fairly represented the condition of society at this time, its spiritual degradation, its subservience to the material side of life. The nineteenth century saw the decomposition of Humanism by itself, the end of the Renaissance, the collapse of the fallacious "reign of man," the final demonstration that he could no longer be a creator after he had set himself up against God. And that is where Socialism came in, because it does not find true human life in man's creative work and the unrestricted use of his proper powers. The Renaissance was aristocratic; it was the work of men who did not admit the supremacy of the necessities of existence. Socialism condemns everything aristocratic to extinction and asserts man's life to be functional to collective labour and an overpowering necessity; every activity must be strictly regularized in the interests of a material whole. The Renaissance was a proclamation of man's rights, of human individuality above all, in science and art, in intellectual life and in politics.

Socialism opposes to the rights of man the rights of collectivity—which is not mankind at large, for it comes before us in a definitely unhuman guise. Even that liberty of thought which was the motive of the Renaissance disappears in collectivism. Every form of thought is under compulsion, controlled by a sectarian social centralization: that is to say that this collectivism is a return to the middle ages, but on a materialistic anti-religious basis. The end of the Renaissance bears witness to the loss of the principle of personality in human societies, of the principle of personal creative initiative, of the principle of personal responsibility; it is a victory for the collective principle.

This passing of the Renaissance can be seen not only in Socialism but as well in Anarchism, not less characteristic of our epoch. Modern history, conceived by the Renaissance, has seen a very great development of the idea of the State; there it differs from the middle ages, which had but a weak consciousness of it. The middle ages were *supra*-nationalist, universalist: the modern ages are a time of national states. At the basis of these new states there is self-affirmation of man, first in the monarchies, then in the democracies, and these humanist national states are doomed to deny themselves. Humanistic Democracy undermines the religious foundation of the State and prepares the conditions for its fall into anarchy. Anarchism means the end of the State—and the State was an achievement of the Renaissance. Anarchism furthermore brings about the self-destruction of the principle of personality—the last unavoidable crash of individualism from the height of its apparent triumph. The principle of personality was closely and inseparably bound up with the principle of the State: Anarchism is the victory of that blind mass-force that is the enemy of both. The anarchist spirit has a vicious hate for all creativeness, it wants to destroy everything that the Renaissance has made: it is a revolt against the lie of Humanism. When societies begin to hanker after equality any kind of renaissance and harvest of creation is at an end. For the principle of equality is one of envy, envy of the being of another and bitterness at the inability to affirm one's own. The passion for equality is a passion for nothingness. Modern societies are in the grip of a passion for displacing the centre of gravity of existence by moving it from what is, by a creative affirmation, the being of each one to an envious denial of the being of another. That is a mark of a senile society.

VIII

The Renaissance began with the affirmation of man's creative individuality; it has ended with its denial. Man without God is no longer man: that is the religious meaning of the internal dialectic of modern history, the history of the grandeur and of the dissipation of humanist illusions. Interiorly divided and drained of his spiritual strength, man becomes the slave of base and unhuman influences; his soul is darkened and alien spirits take possession of him. The elaboration of the humanist religion and the divinization of man and of humanity properly forebodes the end of Humanism. The flowering of the idea of humanity was possible only so long as man had a deep belief in and consciousness of principles above himself, was not altogether cut off from his divine roots. During the Renaissance he still had this belief and consciousness and was therefore not yet completely separated; throughout modern history the European has not totally repudiated his religious basis. It is thanks to that alone that the idea of humanity remained consistent with the spread of individualism and of creative activity. The humanism of Goethe had a religious foundation, he kept his faith in God. The man who has lost God gives himself up to something formless and inhuman, prostrates himself before material necessity.

Nowadays there is none of that "renaissential" play and inter-play of human powers which gave us Italian painting and Shakespeare and Goethe; instead unhuman forces, spirits unchained from the deep, crush man and becloud his image, beating upon him like waves from every side. It is they, not man, who have been set free. Man found his form and his identity under the action of religious principles and energies; the confusion in which he is losing them cannot be re-ordered by purely human efforts. The elaboration of a human universe also was the work of divine influences. Modern man has at the last become separated from the might of God, he spurns his cornerstone, and falls back into chaos. The making of a reservoir of effective energy supposes the preservation of the forms of human identity, the keeping of the boundary-lines which divide man from formless and therefore lower orders. There is a breach in the reservoir, and creative energy pours out and is lost. When man loses his forms and his boundaries there is nothing left between him and the malignant endlessness of a disordered world.

If we trace the ruin of the Renaissance in modernist art, in Futurism, in philosophy, in Critical Gnoseology, in the theosophical and occultist movements, and finally in Socialism and Anarchism, all of which hold an important place in the social life of to-day, we shall also find it in current religious and mystical drifts. In some of them we can see Humanism breaking up from within and dragging down man's form and likeness in its fall; in others a better principle rises above Humanism, and man seeks his salvation at the divine wells of life. But in either case the historical Renaissance is ended in a return to mediaeval principles, either by ways of darkness or by ways of light. Humanism betrayed reality, which is holy, and man pays for this treachery the price of his own history: he suffers disillusion after disillusion.

We are now taking part in the beginnings of the barbarization of Europe; after the refined corruption which marked the highest point of European culture the barbarian invasion has its turn. Herein, we can say with certainty, the World War played a calamitous part in our destinies. Civilized humanist Europe was pillaged and to-day she stands defenceless against savage hordes from both within and without. Smothered underground rumblings had been heard for a long time, but the weak-kneed bourgeois society of Europe did nothing to save its age-long and eternal *holy realities*. We went on carelessly, relying on a prosperity that we never supposed could end. Now night is on us. We are going into a period of senility and decay. There may be a new chaos of peoples; the feudalization of Europe is a possibility. There is no such thing in the history of mankind as a continual progress upward in a straight line, a progress in which the men of the nineteenth century believed so firmly that they made a religion of it; societies and civilizations undergo organic processes which have their periods of youth, maturity, and senescence, of expansion and decay. We are not living to-day so much at the beginning of a new world as at the end of an old one. Our age resembles that of the fall of the Roman empire, the failure and drying-up of Graeco-Roman culture, forever the head-water of all European culture. Modernist art recalls the loss of the old forms of perfection under the barbarian invasions; our social and political activities resemble those under the emperor Diocletian, when man was no longer his own master; religious and philosophico-mystical researches to-day are not unlike the curious examining of the mysteries at the end of Greek philosophy—betraying a hunger for the Incarnation, for the coming of a God-Man. Spiritually, our time is like the Hellenistic age with its universalism and syncretism. A terrible "home-sickness" has taken hold of the better part of mankind. It is a sign of the approach of a new age of religion.

IX

The humanist experiment whose destructive internal dialectic has provided so huge a field of experience for us had to be carried through to the bitter end. All its avenues have now been explored, and we have to look elsewhere, and higher. It is not possible to return to the more simple conditions in which European man lived before the humanist era. The modern age has divided, sharpened, arraigned everything for man, and that is its significance far more than its conquests and positive achievements. Something has been opened out by Humanism, a tremendous problem put before us. Man has had enough of a life cut off from its religious centre, and a quest for a new religious balance, a spiritual deepening, will begin; in no order of his activity can he carry on any longer merely on the surface, a purely external life. He must either go deep or peter-out altogether, and after the trials and shocks he has sustained a deepening seems to be indicated. It is up to European man to shake off humanist illusions once and for all. He cannot live any longer under the rule of the "happy medium," for it leads to a split between the two opposed sides, the higher and the lower. If we may judge from numerous symptoms, we are approaching a new historical epoch, one which will resemble the first middle age, those still obscure seventh, eighth, and ninth centuries that preceded the mediaeval renaissance. And many of us cannot but detect affinities between ourselves and the last Romans. That is a worthy consideration. Did not something like it awake in the newly Christian soul of St. Augustine when Rome was threatened by the upheaval of the barbarians? So now we may look on ourselves as the last faithful representatives of the old Christian culture of Europe, threatened by serious dangers on all sides.

Through this epoch of a new, "civilized," barbarism the unquenchable light must be carried as it was borne aloft before by the Christian Church. The image and likeness of man is revealed and maintained in Christianity alone. The faith freed man from the evil spirits of nature which tormented him in the pagan world, from devil-worship. Only redemption by Christ has enabled man to rise to his feet and to stand upright spiritually; it has ransomed him from the elemental forces to whose power he had fallen and was enslaved. The ancient world elaborated man's form and called forth his creative energy, but human personality was still under the dominion of unregenerate nature, the spiritual man was not yet born. Man's second and spiritual birth was due to Christianity. Humanism itself got its humanness from Christ: antiquity alone was not able to give it. But the development of Humanism separated mankind from God and at the same time itself turned against man to destroy his image, for he is made in the image and likeness of God. When man became content with the image and likeness of nature, to be the natural man only, he returned to the influence of lower powers; he was too weak to resist, and is torn anew by spirits of wickedness. The spiritual centre of human personality is again lost. *Humanism's turning against man is the tragedy of modern times.* It is the cause of the defeat and unavoidable ruin of the Renaissance.

People of to-day are very fond of saying that Christianity has failed and that we can look for no help from that direction. But the fact that Europe has not made its Christianity real, but has distorted and betrayed it, cannot be made into a valid argument against its truth and authenticity. Christ never promised that his reign would be realized on earth, but he did say that his kingdom was not of this world and he did foretell a final privation of faith and love. The "untruth" of those who profess and call themselves Christians is a human untruth, a human betrayal and failure, a human weakness and sinfulness; it is not a Christian, not a divine untruth. The indignation which Catholicism arouses is just when it is directed against the Catholic people; but it is blindly unjust when it is directed against the authentic holy things of the Catholic Church. From the beginning man spoiled Christianity and compromised it by his failures, and now he turns upon it and tries to make it responsible for his own sins and follies. Effective spiritual life is a concern of man as well as of God. It offers man a great freedom, which is itself a great test of his strength of spirit. God himself, if I may put it so, awaits man's help and contribution towards Creation. But we, instead of turning towards him his own image in ourselves and offering him freely the fruits of our creative strength, have wasted and squandered that strength in superficial self-affirmation.

Hence our great distress. It looks as if beauty were

breaking up and dying, as if the free creativeness of man will be henceforth impossible, as if his free individuality has reached its term. Nevertheless, it would be cowardly and lacking in faith to give way to discouragement. Human nature has infinite capacity for regeneration and recovery. Yet we cannot imagine a spiritual rebirth for man and his works otherwise than by a deepening of his Christianity to the extent of a new manifestation of the likeness of Christ in man by faithfulness to the Christian revelation of human personality. In Christianity the study of man is not yet thorough and complete; the content of its Revelation as it touches man has not been fully explored and its wealth developed. That is the significance of the "problem of man" raised by the Humanism which made modern times. Contemporary Europe has been very urgent in the betrayal of the Christian revelation of human personality and has thrown it to the wolves of primary impulse and instinct, thereby insinuating into the heart of her civilization a disorderly principle which can plunge her into a chaos of barbarism. But no upheaval or crude passion can put out the light of God's revelation of man and of the God-Man: the gates of Hell shall never prevail against it. That is why the source of that light will subsist however dense the surrounding darkness. And we must look upon ourselves not only as the last Romans, faithful to the past, to eternal truth and beauty, but also as the watchers for the dawn, looking towards the yet unseen day when the sun of the new Christian renaissance shall rise. Perhaps it will show itself in the catacombs and be welcomed by only a few. Perhaps it will happen only at the end of time. It is not for us to know. But we do know beyond any possibility of error that eternal light and eternal beauty cannot be annihilated by any tempest or in any disorder. The victory of number over goodness, of this contingent world over that which is to come, is never more than seeming. And so, without fear or discouragement, we must leave this day of modern history and enter a mediaeval night. May God dispel all false and deceptive light.

X

I am talking about Europe rather than Russia. Russia has remained outside the great modern humanist movement; she has had no renaissance, for a renaissance-spirit is foreign to her people. Russia was always in a high degree Eastern, and so she still is. The principle of personality has never fully opened out for her, and she has never had an abundant flowering of creative individuality. But the Russians took over the last fruits of European Humanism at the moment of its decay, when it was destroying both itself and the divine image in man.

And no other people has gone to such length in the destruction of that image and of human rights and liberty; nowhere else has there been shown so open an enmity to creativeness, so malicious a hate of all manifestation of human individuality.

This is terrifying for us Russians. We are suffering the ruin of the Renaissance in its worst form when we have not experienced the Renaissance itself and therefore have no grand memory of its richly creative past. None of our great literature is informed with its spirit; we discern in its writings not a plentifulness of power but a sickness of the soul, a tormenting search for a way of escape from damnation. Only in Pushkin is there a touch of the Renaissance, and his spirit did not prevail in Russian literature.

At present we have the anti-Renaissance Futurism—without having had the Renaissance creativeness; we have the anti-Renaissance Socialism and Anarchism—without having lived through the unrestricted growth of a national State; we have the anti-Renaissance movements in philosophy and theosophy—without having known the delight of knowledge. The happiness of living freely among a free mankind has never been ours. That is the unique and bitter destiny of Russia. But we are going to feel keenly the desire and need for a spiritual awakening, we shall have to look for the divine beginnings of man and his works. Is a religious sanction for art, human creation, possible for us? Russian religiousness has never supplied one, but in her religious spirit is the only hope of a spiritual revival in our land. Are we Russians qualified to have any part in a Christian renaissance? Certainly we must first pass through a process of great penitence and purification; and in the name of the Christian idea of man we must burn away the idolatry and superstitions of a lying and destructive Humanism.

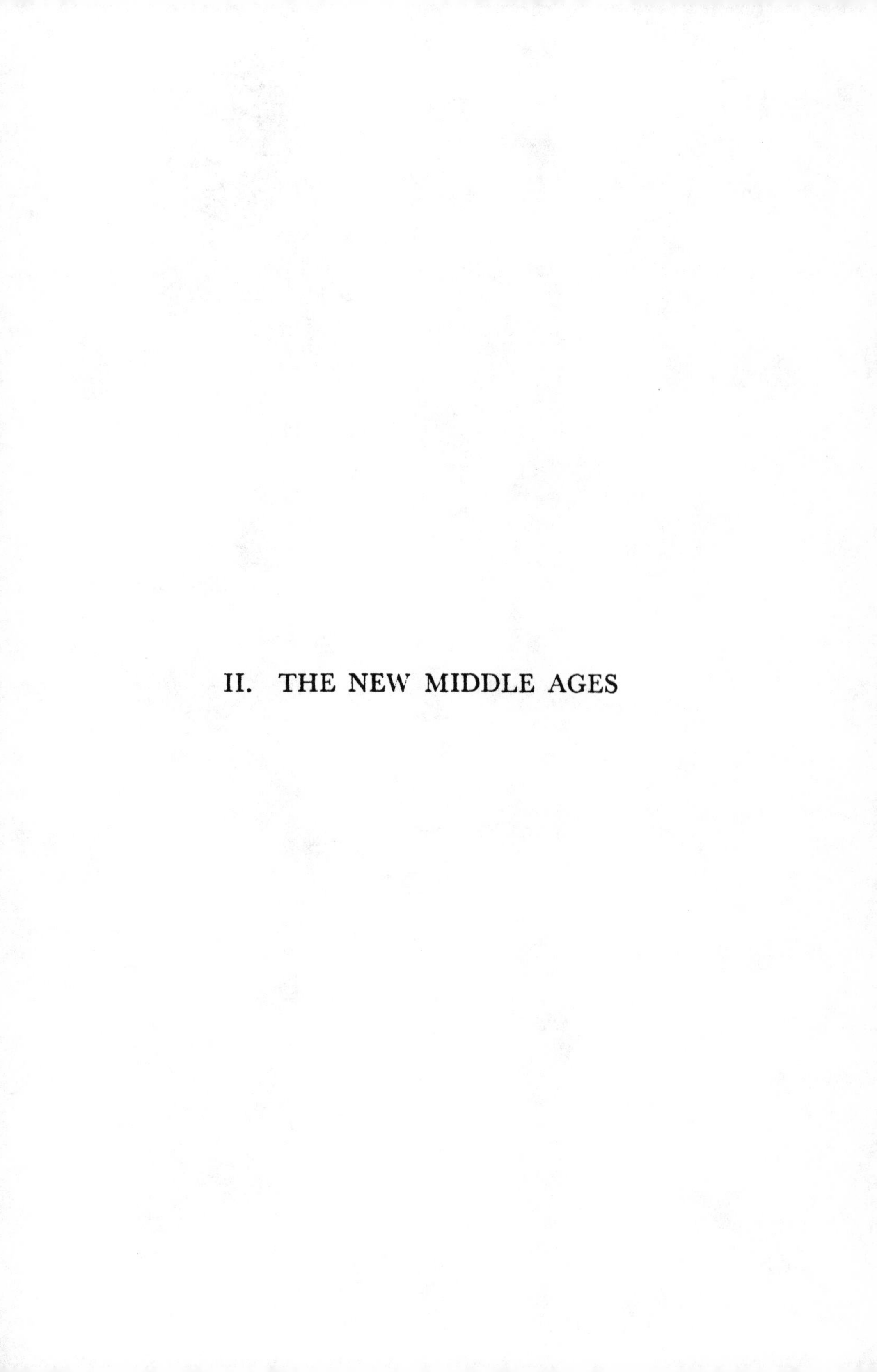

II. THE NEW MIDDLE AGES

II. THE NEW MIDDLE AGES

I

THERE is a rhythm in history as there is in nature, a measured succession of ages and periods, alternation of diverse types of culture, ebb and flow, rise and fall. Such periodicity and rhythm are proper to all life. We can speak of epochs that are organic and of epochs that are critical, of those diurnal and nocturnal, of the sacred times and the secular. It is our lot to live historically in a period of transition. The old world, if I may call it so, or "modern times"—since from habit not less old times are still called modern when they are positively senile—have come to their end and are in decomposition. A new and unknown world is coming to birth. And it is worth noting that this end of one world and beginning of another appears simultaneously to some as a "revolution" and to others as a "reaction." The fact is that revolution and reaction are so inextricably mixed that neither the things nor the terms can well be distinguished from one another. Let us agree that our epoch is the end of modern times and the beginning of a new middle age. I certainly do not mean to foretell the exact course that history will take; I want only to try to point out the characteristics and tendencies which the renewed aspect of society and culture is likely to have.

My ideas are often misinterpreted and I know that people draw the most wrong conclusions from them. The explanation is that my thought is criticized according to current views and attempt is made to bring it into line with such and such a direction of modern thought: this is an essentially wrong way of considering it. The very substance of my philosophy is to have nothing at all to do with the thought of times which, so far as I am concerned, are over and done with. I look to the thought of a world which is to begin, the world of the new middle ages. Contemporary spiritual principles and forces are used up, the rationalist day of a past history declines: its sun sets and night is upon us. The means of research which are adequate to the sun-lit day cannot be of any use for the examination and disentangling of events and phenomena in this eveningtide of history. Men of intuition perceive, all the signs and proofs show, that we have passed from an era of light to an era of darkness. Is it an evil, does this state appear as a misfortune, or are we perhaps pessimistic exaggerators? Such questions are meaningless for they are prompted by a rationalism that is at enmity with the true spirit of history. What is certain is that the veils of falsehood are torn away and we can see both good and evil in their plain nakedness. Night is not less wonderful than day, it is equally the work of God; it is lit by the splendour of the stars and it reveals to us things that the day does not know. Night is closer than day to the mystery of all beginning. The abyss (Jacob Boehme's *Ungrund*) is open only by night: day spreads a veil over it. Tiutchev, the poet of elemental night, has disclosed the mysteries of the mutual relation of the two states:

> This nameless abyss
> is covered with a golden veil
> by the high will of the gods.
> Day is this shining veil. . . . . .
> The night is coming—she is come:
> she strips the blessed pall
> off the ominous world
> and the abyss is there,
> naked, with terrors and with shades,
> nought between us and it.
> So does Night bring us fear.

When twilight falls, shapes lose their clarity and lines their distinction:

> Blue shadows deepen,
> all sound is silent, colours are effaced,
> movement and life die away
> into wavering twilight and distant rumour.

Tiutchev sees in this moment "the hour of wordless longing"; we are living through it, an hour of uncertainty and aching "homesickness," whilst all the veils are thrown aside and the abyss remains uncovered. For Tiutchev night is "holy," and he says of this hour:

> Behold man, without home,
> orphaned, alone, impotent,
> facing the dark abyss;
> all light and life
> are no more than a past dream, far away.
> And in this strange mysterious night
> he sees and knows a fatal heritage.

Night belongs more to metaphysics, to ontology, than does the day. The veil of day, whether in nature or in history, is not fixed and is easily drawn aside. And the whole significance of our epoch, which is a so distressing one for the practical life of individuals, is contained in this clear view of the abyss of Being, in this looking face to face with the principle of life, in this unveiling of the "fatal heritage." That is what going into the night means:

> Like earth-embracing ocean,
> the dream enfolds our life.
> Night comes, and the sounding waves
> break on her shore.
> Her voice calls and invites.
> The bark shudders in the magical haven. . . .
> The flood waxes and bears us on
> to a dark immensity.

Stars in the vault of the sky
look down from the void,
whilst we sail encircled
by the flaming abyss.

WE are in the habit of looking on Tiutchev as a poet of nature and her nocturnal forces. The verses which he has devoted to history are of a different kind, and were written while the light of historical day still subsisted. But he is deeper than we had thought; he is, indeed, a prophet, the prophet and forerunner of the historical night which has overtaken our time. Alexander Blok also will appear later as a poet of this nightfall:

Primeval passions are unloosed
beneath the moon's fatal yoke. . . .

They are not "dawns" that he sees, as Andrew Biely wrongly supposes (he is mistaken in his own views as well), but rather the first shades of night. But neither Blok nor Biely have the key to their own visions, and the interpretation they have given of the event called the "revolution" is wrong. The revolution was not a dawn beginning a new day but the sunset of a day that was done. We are entering a changing period of history: "we sail . . . the flaming abyss . . . the flood waxes . . . a dark immensity."

The light of day can mislead us, the interest of its affairs go stale, its energy slacken, its veils wear out:

then he who has lived on its surface may have a longing for the depths, to reach down to the roots of Being, and the very movement towards profundity, towards an interior life, involves the leaving of daylight, like diving into deep water. St. John-of-the-Cross, that great mystic, speaks of the "dark night of the senses" and "of the soul." The old earthly symbolism of history is insufficient: mankind needs a fresh symbolism that can express what goes on in the depths of the spirit.

An historical day can never give place to night without huge upheavals and ghastly calamities; it does not fade away peacefully. It was thus with the sunset of antiquity, which left behind it an impression of irremediable ruin. The beginning of its new era was marked by a general barbarization: the whole historical order that had built up the past was overrun by a torrent of disordered forces. And here we may well remind ourselves that the most terrible wars and revolutions, wrecking of civilizations, fall of empires, are not due solely to man's ill-will but are also in a measure the work of divine providence. Our age is like to that which saw the passing of the ancient world. Now that was the passing of a culture incomparably finer than the culture of to-day and the civilization of the last century. And in those days people could not yet understand that so marvellous a product of Hellenic culture as Plato might be turned towards the coming night on purpose sooner to leave the Hellenic day. There are still writers of history, Karl Julius Beloch for example, who see in Plato a reaction against the triumphant progress of Greek civilization towards the light. A reaction, maybe. But a reaction that was to last a long time—thousands of years! A reaction, but towards what a future! Dostoievsky was a reactionary of that sort. Let it pass. We can safely say of the new middle ages that they are the night of universal history.

I do not intend this statement in the common sense, "mediaeval darkness," as invented by our modern luminaries, but in a rather deeper, more ontological sense. What I call the new middle ages is the epoch which the rhythm of history brings after that of yesterday: it is the passage from modern rationalism to an irrationalism, or better to a super-rationalism, of the mediaeval type. The wise men of to-day look on all that as obscurantism, a bombination of demons in a pit.* That doesn't matter much. I have a notion that these teachers are very behind the times, that their state of mind is quite reactionary and literally out of date. I am firmly convinced that there is no possibility of a revival or keeping-up of the ways of thought and conception of life which were current before the War and before the calamities which not only Russia but the whole

* The Russian word is untranslatable. It is formed from two words: *mrak*=darkness, and *byesy*=devils—Tr.

of Europe and of the world have undergone. All the usual trends of thought and ways of living adopted by the most "advanced" people and "friends of progress," even of the revolutionaries of the nineteenth and twentieth centuries, are decayed past hope and have no significance for the present time, *a fortiori* for the future. All our terms, words, notions, must be understood in an altered sense, more deep and more ontological; very soon it will be difficult, impossible, to make use of words to which the old qualifications of progress or reaction are attached: they will have to be given their true ontological meaning. The time is coming fast when everyone will have to ask himself whether "progress" was progress or whether it was a most vicious "reaction," a movement away from the meaning of the universe and the authentic foundations of life. We must agree about the words that we use, for the avoidance of utterly useless and idle disputes.

II

Russians love to argue about whether a thing is reactionary or not: no more serious question can engage their attention. It is an old bad habit of the intellectuals, and one would have thought that the revolution would have got them out of it. But no, we still go on with our endless tedious discussions about progress and reaction, just as though everything in the world had not been turned upside down and as though our old criteria had not lost every shred of significance. Just try to judge world-history with reference to reaction or revolution, try to place your "right" and your "left" . . . The absurdity of this sort of thing will strike you immediately and the pathetic procession of your conceptual categories takes on an air of sheer provincialism.

At the time of the fall of the ancient world and the beginning of Christianity it was "reactionary" to defend the principles of civilization and the old culture, and it was in the highest degree "progressive," even revolutionary, to support those spiritual principles of which, later on, mediaeval culture was to be the vindication. Creative activity and spiritual revolution led to the "darkness of the middle ages." It was not the last citizens, writers, and philosophers of antiquity but the Fathers and Doctors of the Church who in those days were the leaders of a true spiritual movement. At the Renaissance, the dawn of modern history, on the contrary, the new fashions were directed back to antiquity and its old principles. Joseph de Maistre, the Romantic Movement of the beginning of last century, was a reaction from the French Revolution and the Enlightenment of the eighteenth; nevertheless, it was the earlier activity that fertilized the thought of the hundred years that followed.

What *can* be properly defined as reactionary is the wish to return to a near past, to a state of mind and set of conditions which governed up to the time of a recent change. Thus it was extremely reactionary to want to go back behind the French Revolution to the material and spiritual organization of the eighteenth century, to the very conditions which had brought about the revolution. But it was not at all reactionary to want to go back to mediaeval principles, to what was eternal in them; people certainly must not go back to that in the past which was temporary and accidental: but to what is eternal, yes. So to-day we must look on as reactionary any return to those modern principles which were definitely in the ascendant in nineteenth century society and which we now see have failed. A call for the crystallization of the principles established in modern times is a call for reaction in the worst sense of the word, it would be a huge obstacle in the path of all creative activity. The old worn-out world to which we can never go back is precisely the world of modern history: a world of rationalist prophets, of individualism and Humanism, Liberalism and democratic theories, of imposing national monarchies and imperialist politics, of a monstrous economic system compounded of Industrialism and Capitalism, of vast technical apparatus, of exterior conquests and practical achievements; a world of unbridled and endless covetousness in its public life, of atheism and supreme disdain for the soul, and, at last, of Socialism, the end and crown of all contemporary history. We gladly echo the words of the revolutionary song, "Down with the old world!" —but we understand by that term this doomed world of modern times.

When we write that some historical world or other is doomed to destruction, naturally we do not mean that nothing will be left of it, that it has nothing meet for eternity, that its very existence was futile. That may not be said of any epoch in history, and modern history was not brought about by chance. It experienced a great tension of human forces and it was a fine experiment in liberty. We do not want to ignore Leonardo or Michelangelo or Shakespeare or Goethe, or any of the other mighty heralds of human freedom. Humanist self-affirmation was a moment of value in the destiny of the human spirit and the lived experience of this self-affirmation has not been wasted: man has gained much from it. The humanist heresy made by modern history contains a distorted truth. The new middle age will give a place to that experiment in liberty made by the modern world, with all the real benefits that we owe to it in the order of consciousness and the increased refining of the spirit that it has brought about. After the middle ages, men failed to effect a return to antiquity but instead accomplished the Renaissance, a very complex association of Christian and pagan elements; in the same way the experience of modern times does not allow us to go back to the old middle ages, but only forward to a new middle age. Léon Bloy used to say, "Suffering passes away, but to have suffered never passes away." Neither the ancient world nor the mediaeval world is perished for ever, though the hour came for both to be superseded. It is just the same now: the world is undergoing a gigantic revolution; not the communist revolution which, at bottom, is everything that is most reactionary, a mess of all the rotten elements of the old world, but a true spiritual revolution. The call to a new middle age is a call to this spiritual revolution, to a complete renewal of consciousness.

In all cultural and social life Humanism is giving way to its opposite, which leads us accordingly to the denial of man's image. The humanist system of ideas is now, to say the least, out of date and reactionary. But there still remain the anti-humanist deductions which the communists have been able to draw from Humanism for adaptation to their own ends. We live in a time of stripping, things can be seen as they are. Look at Humanism stripped naked and observe its nature, which appeared so innocent and good to another age. *Where there is no God there is no man*: that is what we have learned from experience. Or look at the true nature of Socialism, now that we can see what it really looks like. But a truth that stands out and can be seen no less clearly is that there cannot be religious neutrality or absence of religion: to the religion of the living God is opposed the religion of Satan, facing the faith of Christ there is the faith of Antichrist. The neutral humanist kingdom that wanted to establish itself in an order intermediate between Heaven and Hell is in a state of corruption, and the two gulfs, of height above and of depth beneath, are disclosed. There rears up against the God-Man, not the man of the neutral intermediate kingdom, but the man-god, the man who has put himself in the place of God. The opposed poles of Being and of not-being are manifest and clear.

Religion cannot be "each man's private concern," as is enunciated nowadays. It cannot be autonomous any more than can any other category of culture. Real religion is in the highest degree generalized and collective, and holds the first place in a society. Communism proves it: it discards the modern independent and lay systems and demands a "sacred" society, the submission of all phases of life to the religion of Satan and Antichrist. What a colossal significance this has! For herein Communism goes beyond the boundaries of modern history to an entirely different sort of system which I am bound to characterize as mediaeval. The falling to pieces of the humanist "middle-way" lay-state, the emergence everywhere of opposed principles as far apart as the poles, clearly mark the end of the modern non-religious age and the beginning of a religious one, of a new mediaeval period.

I do not mean that the religion of the one God, the faith of Jesus Christ, is going to triumph absolutely and in the order of quantity, but that all aspects of life will be engaged in a religious struggle, grouped under opposed religious principles. This age of deadly warfare between Christianity and Anti-christianity will then not be secular but sacred, and in it the religion of Satan and the spirit of Anti-christ must needs dominate quantitatively. That is why the Communism of Russia and the unfolding of a religious drama in that country already belong to the new middle ages and not to the preceding "modern times."

And in considering Russian Communism we must not rely on the categories of modern history, Humanism, Democracy, or even humanistic socialism, nor may we speak of liberty or equality, understood according to the spirit of the French Revolution. In Bolshevism there is a passing of all bounds, a flood, an agonizing attainment of something most superlative; its tragedy is not enacted in the full day of modern history but in the darkness of mediaeval night. In communist Russia one can travel only by the stars, and to understand the revolution modern astronomy must be put aside for mediaeval astrology. The uniqueness of the Russian destiny resides in the fact that she has never been able wholly to accept humanist culture with its rationalist concepts, formal logic and law, neutrality in religion, and general secular compromise; she has never left the sacred epoch of the middle ages entirely behind her and has, so to speak, jumped from what remained of those ages and their theocracy right into the new middle ages and their satanocracy. Humanism in Russia has expressed itself only in the fixed forms of "homodeism," in such figures as Dostoievsky's Kirilov, Piotr Verhovensky, and Ivan Karamazov, and not at all in accordance with the humanist spirit of the West. And that is why a very special part will be assigned to Russia in the passing from modern history to the new middle ages: she is more likely to give birth to Antichrist than to a humanistic democracy and a laicized neutral culture.

III

The approach to the new middle age, like the approach to the old one, is marked by a visible rotting of old societies and an invisible formation of new ones. Was the failing but tenacious modern order really "cosmic"? The nineteenth century was very proud of its law, its constitutions, the unity of its method and its scientific paraphernalia. But it is an interior unity that is conclusive, and this it did not realize: it was infected by individualism, by "atomism." Throughout modern history society has been eaten away by a series of internal maladies, man turning against man and class against class: all societies have been characterized by the warfare of opposing interests, by competition, by the isolation and dereliction of each individual man. An ever-growing anarchy may be justly pointed out in the spiritual and intellectual life of these societies, a radical lesion due to the loss of a true centre or of the vision of a one supreme end. Such loss conditioned the autonomy of all intellectual and social spheres as well as the secularization of society at large.

The modern spirit thought that freedom lay in individualism, in the right for each man and each cultural activity to decide for himself. We have gone so far as to call the process of modern history a process of emancipation. But emancipation *from* what and *for* what? From the old authoritarian theocracies, from the old idea of dependence? Those theocracies could no more subsist, and as for the old heteronomy, it was necessary that it should be got rid of; I do not claim for a minute that freedom of spirit was other than an indefeasible and eternal acquisition. But why and in view of what did there have to be an emancipation? Modern times have no answer to give. And in the name of whom, in the name of what? In the name of man, of Humanism, of the freedom and happiness of mankind? . . . The answer is not there. Man cannot be set free in the name of man's freedom, for man cannot be the last end of man. We are faced with complete nothingness. If there is nothing towards which man can lift up his eyes he is deprived of substance. In that case human liberty is simply a formula without any content, and individualism is in essence a negative reform whose development can bring no help to anybody.

Individualism is founded on no eternal principle, it has nothing ontological about it; least of all can it strengthen personality and set off the image of man. In an individualistic age notable "individualities," strong personalities, do not flourish at all. The individualistic civilization of last century, with its democracy and materialism, its technique, its public opinion, its press, its stock-exchange and parliament, did much to bring low and kill personality, to enfeeble individuality, and to produce a general levelling-down and "mixing." Personality was grander and more striking during the mediaeval centuries. Individualism has helped on the equalitarian movement which wipes out all differentiation between individualities; it has led to a sort of "atomization" of society and so to Socialism, which is only the reverse of breaking-down into atoms, a mechanical and artificial amalgam of them. The idea of universality so characteristic of the middle ages has ceased to have any influence in ours. It is only when human personality is rooted in the universal, in the cosmos, that it finds an ontological ground to give it its chief substance. Personality exists only where God and the divine are recognized; otherwise individualism wrenches personality from its seed-plot, pulls it apart, and scatters it to the winds of chance. Individualism has exhausted all its possibilities and energy, it can rouse nobody to enthusiasm.

This also contributes to the end of modern history: all the attempts—interior, not exterior—to overcome individualism were so many breaches in its defences. Among those who opposed individualistic anarchy was Auguste Comte, who thereby manifested the mediaeval side of his mind, but he followed a completely unnatural formula. As things are we can regard individualism only as utter reaction, though it still flatters itself that it is the pioneer of liberty, light, and progress. Liberalism, parliamentarism, constitutionalism, juridical formalism, rationalism and empirical philosophy, so many fruits of the individualist spirit and of humanist self-affirmation, are all reactionary, they have had their day and their original significance is played out. All these forms lose the sharpness of their outline in the twilight of modern history: man's atmosphere is now universal and cosmic, he meets the mystery of life and finds himself faced with God. He was chained to individualism by forms which cut him off from other men and from the world at large. Now he moves towards generality, an epoch of universality and collectivity. He no longer believes that he was self-sufficient and could look after himself from the moment that he had rationalist thought, lay morality, Law, Liberalism, Democracy and Parliaments. Too many things testify to the contrary, the strifes which disturb mankind, the wholesale divisions, the absence of a common spirit, in which may be recognized the effects of legalized *mésalliances*, of negotiations for mutual peace and respective isolation, and of everybody's unconcern about the choice of a truth. Rationalism, Humanism, Law, Liberalism, Democracy, all these are forms of life and thought which at bottom take the hypothesis that Truth is unknowable and perhaps does not exist: in other words, they do not want to know the truth.

Holy Truth is union and not disunion, and it is not a limitation; nor is it concerned above all to maintain man's right to err, to deny and outrage Truth, although Truth itself includes liberty. But what is humanist Democracy if not an assertion of a right to error and falsehood, a political relativism, a sophistry, a giving-over of the decision of truth to the votes of a majority? And what is rationalist philosophy if not an entire confidence in the individual reason, fallen though it be from the height of Truth and cut off from the sources of being?—moreover, an affirmation of a right in thought not to *want* to choose truth or to look to it for the ability to know. What is Parliament if not the legislative-assembly of discord, the holding of "opinion" above "knowing" (I use these words in a platonic sense), unable to go forward to a life of truth? Truth must be accepted freely and not under constraint, it will not allow slave-relations with itself: Christianity teaches that. But modern history has for long been wedded to a theoretical liberty to accept Truth, to a liberty that had no free choice, and that is why it has made up ways of thought and life that are founded not upon Truth but on the right to choose no matter what truth or lie, which means the creation of a culture and a society without an object because they do not know in the name of what they exist.

So has been brought about this latter time when men prefer not-being to Being, and as man is not able to serve and live for himself alone he makes false gods, if he does not know the true God. He has been unwilling to receive the liberty of God and perforce has fallen into a cruel bondage to deified deceits, to idols. He has been without freedom of spirit and it is not in the name of liberty that the man of the end of this age rises in revolt and denies Truth. He is in the power of an unknown master, of a superhuman and inhuman force that grips the society that does not want to know Truth, the holy truth of God. Only in Communism have we been able to learn something about the tyranny of this master. Nevertheless, it has already made what I have called a breach in the defences of modern history. We must choose. Liberty as a formula, as now understood, is discredited; it is imperative that we go on to its substance, to true liberty.

States and cultures are collapsing because they were upreared on that nineteenth-century philosophy which has broken down. Monarchical and democratic governments are alike involved, because they alike had their origins in Humanism, but it is not such or such form of state that is crashing but the State itself. There is no solid and durable form of polity left: no government can be sure to-day that it will still be to-morrow. No "legitimism," whether of the old monarchies or of the young sovereignties of the people, retains its hold over men. Nobody now believes in any juridical or political form or would give a ha'penny for a constitution. The force of reality prevails against everything else. Ferdinand Lassalle spoke the truth in his remarkable *Discourse upon the Constitution.* The bases of a government are not juridical, they are socio-biological. The World War proved this once for all when it destroyed faith in the value of law.

Italian Fascism attests the crisis not less than does Communism. In this system spontaneous assemblies of social groups in effect supersede the old government and take upon themselves the organization of authority. The voluntary fascist army and police are set up beside the official army and police, and in practice control them. This state of affairs also is reminiscent of the fall of the Roman empire and what followed. Fascism is the sole innovation in contemporary European politics and it belongs to a middle age as much as does Communism. It is absolutely contrary to any idea of legitimism, which it does not recognize; it is an unconstrained manifestation of the will to live and to direct, a manifestation, not of law, but of biological energy. We must agree that this practical blow to the legitimist principle, whether monarchical or democratic, its supersession by a principle of force in the insurgence of suddenly united groups, is typical of a new middle age. Fascism does not know in what name it acts, but it abandons juridical forms for life itself.

Rationalist philosophy and formalist knowledge founded on gnoseology have lost their influence in the same way. Gnoseology is exactly juridical supremacy in the order of knowing, legitimism. We see all thought of the day moving towards a vital philosophy of life: it is drawn by an object. Can we not here detect a kind of fascism? Philosophical thought does not know in what name it acts, but it passes from form to substance, from the problem of the legality of the law of knowledge to that of knowledge of life and Being itself. The influence of official and academical philosophy diminishes in the same measure as the influence of parliamentarian politics. These are symptoms of a homogeneous movement whose end is a fellowship of life. The world is in confusion, and it tends towards the construction of a spiritual order analogous to that of the middle ages. Decay precedes a middle age, and it is needful to mark the course of those elements that are dying and those that are coming to birth. But it is well continually to remind ourselves that man, by reason of the power of freedom innate in him, has two ways before him, and that his future is double. Without losing sight of this doubleness I would like to make an attempt to trace out the route which mankind must follow.

IV

Individualism, the "atomization" of society, the inordinate acquisitiveness of the world, indefinite over-population and the endlessness of people's needs, the lack of faith, the weakening of spiritual life, these and other are the causes which have contributed to build up that industrial capitalist system which has changed the face of human life and broken its rhythm with nature. The power of the machine and the chronic "speeding-up" that it involves have created myths and phantoms and directed man's life towards these figments which, nevertheless, give an impression of being more real than realities. But is there in fact so much reality, in the sense of being, ontological reality, in their stock-exchanges, banks, paper-money, monstrous manufactories of useless things or of weapons for the destruction of life, in the ostentation of their luxury, the oratory of their politicians and men-of-law, their newspaper-journalism? Is there so much reality in the progressive increase of our insatiable wants? We see malignant endlessness everywhere, an endlessness that has a horror of solutions.

The whole economic system of Capitalism is an offshoot of a devouring and overwhelming lust, of a kind that can hold sway only in a society that has deliberately renounced the Christian asceticism and turned away from Heaven to give itself over exclusively to earthly gratifications. It is quite obvious that Capitalism is unthinkable as a "sacred" economy. It is the result of a secularization of economic life, and by it the hierarchical subordination of the material to the spiritual is inverted. The autonomy of economics has ended in their dominating the whole life of human societies: the worship of Mam mon has become the determining force of the age. And the worst of it is that this undisguised "mammonism" is regarded as a very good thing, an attainment to the knowledge of truth and a release from illusions. Economic materialism formulates this to perfection when it brands the whole spiritual life of man as a deception and a dream.

Socialism is only a more consistent development of this system, the definitive victory and diffusion of principles latent in it. Socialists take over from bourgeois capitalist society its materialism, its atheism, its cheap prophets, its hostility against the spirit and all spiritual life, its restless striving for success and amusement, its personal selfishness, its incapacity for interior recollection. Waning of the human spirit and disappearance of spiritual creation wait alike on Capitalism and on Socialism, and from this point of view they are seen to be the fine flower of a long historical process of separation of man from God. All energy is concentrated outwardly: that is the change from "culture" to "civilization." All the sacred symbolism of culture dies.

This state of things is nothing new; it could be found in the ancient cultures, and did not the prophets of the Old Dispensation bring the charge? But how much finer, more spiritual, more "otherworldly" were the cultures of old Egypt and of the middle ages compared with that of Western Europe during the past two hundred years. It is an incontestable fact that in contemporary history, so proud of its progress, the centre of gravity of existence is shifted from the spiritual to the material side, from the interior life to the exterior: society gets less and less religious. Life is not dominated and controlled by the Church but by the Stock Exchange; the people at large do not understand, much less are ready to fight and die for, any sacred symbol; men no longer discuss the dogmas of the Faith, they do not live on Christian doctrine, the divine Mysteries mean nothing to them: they consider themselves emancipated from that "holy folly of the Cross."

But there are many signs that this capitalist-socialist period is over. There is the debility of Industrial Capitalism itself. The World War and its unexampled horror was a child of that system; modern imperialism was nourished in its womb, and now feeds on its own entrails. The Capitalism of Europe has been ruined by its militarism. The working-classes used to live under the spell of industrialism, but the war broke the spell. It will be difficult to drive the people back to the pre-war discipline of work which prevailed in capitalist society and to re-establish the old standard of production. Socialism can't do it. The question of the discipline of work is vital for contemporary societies; the old underlying reasons for work have gone and new ones have not been found: but again it is a question of the hallowing and the justifying of work, and is therefore ignored by both Capitalism and Socialism, neither of which is interested in work as such. In order to be able to go on living it is possible that the bankrupt peoples will have to enter on a new path of self-denial, by curbing their covetousness and putting a check on the indefinite expansion of their wants, and by having smaller families. This would be a new asceticism and the negation of industrial-capitalist principles. That, of course, does not mean any denial or handicapping of man's initiative and technical genius but represents the measure of his calling, his obedience to his own human *spirit*. By this path we should be obliged to revive rural economy and return to trades, organizing ourselves into economic associations and trade corporations. The town will have to link up with the country again, and competition be replaced by co-operation. The principle of private property will be kept as an eternal foundation, but it will be limited and spiritualized in application: no more of those scandalous huge private fortunes with which we are so familiar. There will be no pretence at equality, but neither will there be avoidable hunger and poverty. We shall have to have a much more simple and elementary material culture and a spiritual culture that is far more complex.

The end of Capitalism is the end of modern history and the beginning of the new middle ages. The imposing humanist enterprise has failed and the remains ought to be scrapped. But first of all perhaps technical civilization will try the experiment of developing itself to its uttermost limits, till it becomes a diabolical sorcery just as Communism has done. . . . . .

V

Modern history has brought forth forms of nationalism of which the mediaeval world knew nothing. Nationalist movements and separatisms in the West are found to have been the result of the Reformation and of Protestant particularism. The spirit of Catholicism could never have led to such separatism, to such excessive national self-affirmation as has formed itself into self-sufficient national monads (in the same way that human individualities have become self-sufficient monads). It has meant the "atomization" of Christendom; the individualities of nations and the individualities of isolated men ceased to be aware that they were parts of an organic and real whole : each rung claims to be independent of the ladder. The Reformation and Humanism have provided an exclusive affirmation of self as spiritual foundation, and by shutting each one up within himself they have ruined the idea of universality. Religion itself has taken the form of a national enclosure; there is no unity or response to the cosmic unity in Christianity; even the mentality of Catholics has taken on the appearance of being one of these closed-up forms.

Modern nationalism springs from individualism. But if we look at things more closely we shall have to admit that all the movements characteristic of modern history, and among them that of national independence, derive from the victory of nominalism over mediaeval realism. Nationalities end by being decomposed into classes, parties, *et cetera*. The progressive elaboration of national individualism has assuredly had a very great positive importance: it has enriched the real personalities of the nations, made them conscious of themselves, and shown their energy. But the forms of nationalism to which peoples had arrived in the nineteenth and twentieth centuries and which brought on the World War manifest the catastrophe that has befallen mankind, the break-up of spiritual unity, the resurgence of pagan polytheism over Christian monotheism. The present-day nationalism of France, Germany, England, Italy, is all more or less pagan, anti-Christian, anti-religious; French nationalism of the Third Republic is in a high degree a product of atheism. Faith in the living God is waning rapidly, and men have made for themselves a false god, the nation, or worship an even worse idol, internationalism.

A nation has really an ontological basis (which internationalism has not), but it must not be put in the place of God. The Germans have come to believe in a German god. But the German god is not the God of Christians; it is a pagan deity, like the Russian god. In the eyes of the God of Christians, who is the One God, there is neither Greek nor Jew. The Christian religion came into the world and conquered it in an atmosphere of universalism when it built up a unified body of men and women across the world of Hellenic culture and Roman imperialism; its very existence betokened release from nationalism and pagan particularism. Now, at the end of modern times, we behold anew an insurgence of this particularism, and an all-destroying war to the death is being waged at the heart of the world. But this is only one aspect of the matter; there is another.

We are entering on an epoch which at many points makes one think of the age of Hellenic universalism. If there have never been seen such divisions, and consequently such enmities, there have on the other hand never been seen, at least throughout the course of modern history, similar *rapprochements* and attempts at world-unification. For the murderous strife of the war has contributed to a coming-together and fraternizing among the peoples, to the unifying of races and cultures; it drew Russia out of its state of isolation; nationalities are ceasing to keep themselves apart from one another; and this is in accordance with their destiny, all will have to depend upon all. To-day the organization of each people affects the state of the whole world; what happens in Russia has repercussions in every country and upon every race. There has never before been such close contact between the Eastern and the Western worlds, which have lived so markedly separate. Civilization is ceasing to be european and becoming "of the world": Europe will have to renounce her pretension to a monopoly of culture. And Russia, situated midway of East and West, in a terrible catastrophic way has taken on the most considerable significance of all nations: the eyes of the whole world are on her.

Even before the war the ominous dialectic of imperialism had damaged the self-contained national existence of states and forced their people to cross the seas to all parts of the world. The supremacy of Capitalism has brought about an economic world-system and made the economic life of each country dependent on the economic situation in general. This means a very far-reaching economic *rapprochement* between peoples, so that it can be said that a kind of internationalism is native to Capitalism. From the other side, Socialism quickly took on an international character, and in international Communism a new and vicious version of the old idea of compulsory universalism has arisen. The modern world, rent by the violent quarrels of countries, classes, and individuals, prone to suspicion and hate, is yet drawn from every side towards a universal unification, to a conquest over that national exclusivism which has been responsible for the fall of nations. Europe not only received blow after terrific blow during the war but has been weakened ever since by the incessant quarrelling between France and Germany and by the reciprocal suspicion and ill-will of other countries. These absolutely refuse to look to anv common supreme spiritual tribunal. Nevertheless, if we examine deeply enough there certainly can be discerned a stirring towards a world-wide unification more vast than a unified Europe. Internationalism is a despicable caricature of universalism, and the universalist spirit must be rekindled among Christians, they must have and express a will for a free universalism. The Russian people is by nature the most universalist of all the peoples of the world, the quality is part of the very framework of their national spirit, and their calling ought to be to work for world-unification and the formation of a single spiritual cosmos. But for that they would naturally have to be a strong national individuality, whereas actually they are at the mercy of horrible and strongly opposed temptations: to an exclusive internationalism destructive of Russia, and to a not less exclusive nationalism separating Russia from the rest of Europe.

Those movements whose object it is to surmount national barriers and unify the world abandon the individualistic spirit of the end of modern history and inaugurate the new middle age. In that sense, communist internationalism is a phenomenon of that age rather than of the old "modern history," and to that same age must be referred the desire for religious unity (the reunion of the separated parts in Christianity) and for a much wider spiritual culture, both of which are making themselves strongly felt among Christians. I don't mean to say that the new middle ages will be so peaceful that they will know no wars; an enormous struggle may even now be imminent, and we ought to be ready for it. But the wars will not be so much national and political as religious and spiritual.

VI

The disciples of "progress" cannot bear any suggestion of a return to the ideas of the middle ages and zealously oppose any tendencies which they consider mediaeval. This has always surprised me. Firstly, they do not believe at all in the vitality of the beliefs which are associated with the mediaeval spirit, still less in the possibility of their triumph; they are convinced of the solidity and lastingness of the principles of modern history. Then why so much excitement? Secondly, it should be made clear once for all that there never has been and there never will be any return to past times, their restoration is impossible. When we speak of passing from modern history to the middle ages it is a figure of speech; such passage can take place only to a new middle age, not to the old one. That is why such an event should be considered as a revolution of the spirit, an anticipated creative activity, and not at all as the "reaction" that it seems to the "progressives," who are frightened because their own cause is so deteriorated. Moreover, it is time that people stopped talking of the "darkness of the middle ages" in contrast with the "light" of modern history; such talk represents views which are too thin, if I may say so, to be worthy of the level of contemporary historical scholarship. There is no need to idealize the middle ages as the romantics did. We know their negative and truly dark aspects quite well: brutality, roughness, cruelty, violence, serfdom, ignorance of nature, fear in religion bound up with the horror of hell-fire. But we also know that the mediaeval times were truly and eminently religious, that they were carried along by a longing for the vision of God which brought the people to the verge of a holy madness; we know that their whole culture was directed towards that which is transcendent and "beyond," that they owed their Scholasticism and mysticism, to which they looked for the resolution of the supreme problems of being, to a high tension of the spirit to which modern history has no equivalent. Those ages did not waste on exterior things energy that could be concentrated on interior: they hammered out personality in the forms of the monk and the knight; it was in those barbarous days that the cult of the *belle dame* flourished and the *trouvères* and *troubadours* sang their songs. God grant that these traits may again appear in the new middle ages.

In reality the mediaeval civilization was a renaissance in opposition to the barbarism and darkness which had followed the fall of the civilization of antiquity, a chaos in which Christianity alone had been the light and the principle of order. For long it was believed that this complex and rich period had been a great void in the intellectual history of mankind and of its philosophical thought, when as a matter of fact these centuries had so many excellent thinkers and such diversity in the realm of their thought that nothing like it can be found at any other epoch; the things which were substantial and living for them are counted as superfluous luxuries in modern times. A return to the middle ages is then a return to a better religious type, for we are far below their culture in the spiritual order; and we should hurry back to them the more speedily because the movements of negation in our decadence have overcome the positive creative and strengthening movements. The middle ages was not a time of darkness, but a period of night; the mediaeval soul was a "night-soul" wherein were displayed elements and energies which afterwards shut themselves up within themselves at the appearing of this weary day of modern history.

What will the new middle age look like to us? It is easier to catch its negative than its positive characteristics. It is before all, as I have already said, the end of Humanism, of individualism, of formal liberalism, and the beginning of a new religious collectivity in which opposing forces and principles will be defined and everything which is concealed in the underground or subconsciousness of modern history will be laid bare. The rotting humanist kingdom is dividing into two parts: an extreme Communism, anti-human and atheist, and that Church of Christ who is called to receive within herself all authentic being. There is the passage from the formalism of modern history which, after all, has chosen nothing, neither God nor devil, towards discovering the object of life. All the autonomous activities of civilization and social life are reduced to nothingness, the impetus of independent secular creation is spent, and longing is awakened in all spheres of activity for a religious choice, for a real existence, for a transfiguration of life.

None of the spheres of creation and aspects of culture and social life can remain neutral, which means definitely secular, in the matter of religion. Philosophy does not intend to be the handmaid of theology, or society to recognize the authority of an ecclesiastical hierarchy. But at the heart of knowledge and of social life a will to religion is quickening. Forms of knowledge and of society must spring from within, flowing from the freedom of a religious spirit, and a tendency towards theurgy has shown itself in art. There is no possibility of a revival of the old theocracy and of the former heteronomous relations between religion and the different aspects of life. In past theocracy the Kingdom of God was never actualized but only signified by outward symbols. Now there is everywhere a will *really* to attain the Kingdom of God, or the kingdom of Satan; a will, that is, for a free "rule-by-God," distinct from both "rule-by-self" and "rule-by-another."

Knowledge, morality, art, the State, economics, all must become religious, not by external constraint but freely and from within. No theology can regulate the process of my knowledge from outside and impose a norm: knowledge is free. But I cannot any longer realize the ends of knowledge without adverting to religion and undergoing a religious initiation into the mysteries of Being. In that I am already a man of the middle ages and no more a man of modern history. I do not look for the autonomy of religion, but for liberty in religion. No ecclesiastical hierarchy can now rule and regulate society and the life of the State, no clericalism is able to make use of external force. Nevertheless I cannot re-create the State and a decayed society otherwise than in the name of religious principles. I do not look for the autonomy of the State and of society in regard of religion, but for the foundation and strengthening of State and society *in* religion. Not for anything in the world would I be free from God; I wish to be free *in* God and *for* God. When the flight from God is over and the return to God begins, when the movement of aversion from God becomes a movement towards Satan, then modern times are over and the middle ages are begun. God must again be the centre of our whole life—our thought, our feeling, our only dream, our only desire, our only hope. It is needful that my passion for a freedom without bounds should involve a conflict with the world, but not with God.

The crisis of our actual culture began long ago. Revolution begins within before it declares itself openly, and now wars, revolutions, and other disasters have outwardly manifested the interior crisis. Culture is by its nature symbolic: I mean to say that it creates spiritual values in the present life which are the *sign* of a life to come, of an eternal life of which our earthly life is only the preparation and figure. Culture can only indicate this spiritual life by signs (I am not speaking of the hidden life of souls), it cannot see it really and immediately. This symbolical nature of culture often escapes those who are enslaved by its traditional forms; it is usually perceived only by the "symbolist-minded," who tend to reach higher and touch the reality of the spiritual world. Thus historical theocracy was only symbolic and achieved the signs but not the earthly reality of the Kingdom of God. But the men who established theocracy did not understand that this was so and that is why they regarded it with so much reverence. Those who apprehend religious symbolism necessarily draw nearer to the actualization of the Kingdom of God, that is, to a genuine transfiguration of life. Knowledge, art, morality, the State, even the outward life of the Church, did not effect this and did not properly attain to being; they could only produce symbols of transfiguration and signs of a being that is more than real.

It is just this sacred symbolism in which the grandeur and beauty of culture were made visible that the modern world has ruined; nineteenth and twentieth-century civilization refuses it and wants itself to make a real life. To this end it has elaborated its formidable technique. On the one hand, the crisis of culture comes from the demand of a realist civilization for life and power; on the other, it is associated with the emergence of a religious will which aspires to transfigure life, to attain new being, to make a new heaven and a new earth. This will to a complete reality, a truly ontological will moving towards unity and integrity, is not satisfied with divided and self-sufficient cultural activities. But along with the crisis of which I have spoken degeneration overtakes the age-long forms of culture, art, philosophy, *et cetera.* Nowadays, intellectual life has no visible and recognized spiritual centre. The University has lost this position and with it all spiritual authority; neither academical philosophy nor academical art have any living influence; the leaders of modern thought are not found among the dons. It is the same with parliamentarian politics; they are quite out of touch with life. Vital processes make themselves felt spontaneously, not through the official channels.

The spiritual centre in the near future will be, as in the old middle ages, the Church alone. Her life is developing unseen, outside official lines, for her boundaries are not clearly marked and cannot be pointed out as if they were a material object. The life of the Church is a mystery and her ways cannot be understood by reason alone: the Spirit breatheth where he will, and creative movements appear which, from the external, official, simply rationalist point of view, seem strange and foreign to the Church. The crisis of culture means that, where religion is concerned, it cannot maintain a humanist neutrality but must inevitably become either an atheist and anti-Christian civilization or else a sacred culture animated by the Church, a transformed Christian life. The last supposes a creative movement in the Church, a more complete showing forth of Christian truth about man and his calling in the world, a full manifestation of the mystery of creation and cosmic life. The Christianity of the oecumenical councils and the great doctors has not yet sufficiently expounded the truths about man and the universe. The Church is cosmic by her nature and contains within herself the fullness of Being; she is the universe baptized. This ought to be a living and practical truth instead of just a theoretical and abstract doctrine; and the Church must pass from the period in which the sanctuary has predominated to a period of transfiguration of the cosmic fullness of life. Modern religion has become merely a department of culture, with a special place reserved for it—a very small one. It must again become *all*, the force which transfigures and irradiates the whole of life from within: its spiritual energy must be set free to renew the face of the earth.

Christianity has reached a stage in which the intellect will play an increasingly important part, as it did in the days of the great teachers beginning with Clement of Alexandria. The "people" are being led away from the faith by atheistic propaganda and by Socialism; but the "intellectuals" are coming back to it. And that is having a considerable effect on Christianity.

VII

The new middle ages will vanquish the "atomism" of modern history; it is, indeed, already beaten in a false fashion by Communism, truly by the Church and the oecumenical spirit. The new middle age, like the old, is hierarchical in structure, whereas modern history everywhere repudiates such an organization. Man is not a unit in the universe, forming part of an unrational machine, but a living member of an organic hierarchy, belonging to a real and living whole. The very idea of personality is bound up with hierarchy, while "atomism" destroys its fundamental character. An unconstrained return to hierarchical principles is everywhere inevitable; they alone bear witness to the universal harmony of creation. Communism itself, anti-individualist, anti-liberal, anti-democratic, anti-humanist, is hierarchical in its way; it denies modern formal liberties and equalities and builds up its satanist order of subordination, a false church, a communion of lies. It is no good opposing to this the anti-hierarchical humanist, liberal, and democratic ideas; it can be fought only by another hierarchy, but one ontologically founded, an organic and real communion.

The old conservative and monarchical ideas, called "of the right," which held sway in certain countries before the war and the revolution were at bottom individualistic ideas; they were sustained by an aristocratic humanism, in the same way that a democratic humanism was at the root of the ideas of "the left" or the "progressives." Humanist self-affirmation is found as much involved in the monarchies of Louis XIV and Louis XV as in those of William II and the tsars. Against the aristocratic humanist affirmation of self there is always the democratic humanist affirmation of self, absolute democracy arises against absolute monarchy. The emperor or the nobility have no more right to power than the people, peasants or industrial workers. In general, there is no human right to power and all desire of power is a sin, and the sin in this kind flaunted by a Louis XIV or a Nicholas I is comparable with that of Robespierre or of Lenin. Power is a duty and not a right; it is a just power, not when it is claimed in its own name or in that of the claimants, but only when it is rightly claimed in the name of God alone, in the name of Truth.

Modern times look on power as a right and are much concerned with fixing the bounds of that right. The new middle ages will look on power as a duty, and political life founded on a scramble for the right to power will be stigmatized as unreal and parasitical, without ontological significance. Nine-tenths of politics is lies, deceit, sham. At the most a tenth of it has one element of reality: the organization of that power without which the world cannot go on, that is, the power of God. Faith in all kinds of politics is already much shaken, political activity does not play the part it used to, and the time is coming for it to give place to more real spiritual and economic processes. The "hierarchism" natural to life will come back, and those who are endowed with great realist force will take the place for which they are qualified: life cannot prosper without a spiritual aristocracy. The method of "direct action" and the spontaneous activity of individual personalities and groups show that the call to overturn the old politics has been heard: but they have produced only reflexes and must give way before the urgent requirements of real life. Political parties and their leaders will certainly lose their apparent importance —such parties do not produce men of worth, "good men"; and parliaments must definitely be got rid of: their life is fictitious, they are parasitical growths on the body politic, incapable of fulfilling any organic function. The stock-exchange and the press will no longer be masters of the world. Social life will be simplified; making an honest living will require a lower standard and less artificiality. It is likely that men will form themselves into unified groups, not under political emblems, which are always secondary and generally counterfeit, but under economic tokens of immediate importance, according to professional categories of trade, art, and other work, spiritual and material; these will take the place of the present castes and classes. There is a great future before professional unions, co-operative gilds, corporations in general, and they are a clear indication of the middle ages on a new basis. Instead of political "talking-shops" we shall have assemblies of professionals representing real bodies, not intriguing for political power but bent upon dealing with vital matters—for themselves and not in the interests of parties. Future society will be of the syndicalist type, but understood in a very different sense from that of revolutionary syndicalism. The only polity that has any worth is that wherein a very decided radicalism observes the hierarchical principles of power. There is some truth even in Anarchism in so far as it is an enemy of state-domination and of exaggerated ascendancy of governmental functions.

The new middle ages will be, inevitably and in the highest degree, "of the people"—and not in the least democratic. Already the toiling millions and the huge middle-classes play a very great part in the fortunes of governments; all politics of the future will have to take them into account and find measures to neutralize the dangers to qualitative culture arising from the influence of "the masses." But this does not at all mean that the great body of the people will get political power through democracy, universal suffrage, and such like expedients. The Russian revolution has shown clearly that the people at large by no means always seek to express their social sense through democracy. Democracies are inseparable from middle-class domination and the industrial-capitalist system. The masses ordinarily are indifferent to politics, for they never have enough strength to seize power. A far more likely conjecture is that the peasants and industrial-workers, on whom the burdens of social life bear more and more heavily, will look to corporate professional representation on the *soviet* principle, but in the true meaning of that word ("council") and not according to the fiction which covers the dictatorship of the Communist Party in "Soviet Russia." It will be the business of these social unions to save the State and society from ruin; these living associations, professional, economic and spiritual, will *be* the society and the State of the new middle ages. It is the spiritual and material needs of the people that clamour to be satisfied, not their aspirations after power. Power has never belonged and can never belong to a great number; to be so is not in accordance with its nature, which is hierarchical, and its structure is hierarchical too. So it will be in the future: the people cannot govern itself, it must be governed, and that means having governors. In republics and other democracies the governors are a tiny minority of political leaders, bankers, newspaper-proprietors, and such like. So-called popular sovereignty is only a moment in the life of a people, when its instinctive might overflows. The structure of a state and the constitution of its social order should always display inequality and hierarchy and lodge sovereignty only in a determined *part* of the body politic.

It is by no means impossible that the unity of societies and states in the new middle ages will express itself in monarchical forms. The masses themselves are quite capable of recognizing their leaders and heroes and wanting a king. But these monarchies would naturally be of a new pattern, different from that of modern history and nearer the mediaeval type: "Caesarism" would be the strongest characteristic. I have thought for a long time that we are getting near, especially in Russia, to an original form which might be called "soviet-monarchy," syndicalist monarchy, monarchy with a new social complexion. The old royalist legitimism is dead; it belonged to another age, and to seek its restoration is to run after a ghost. The monarchies of the new middle ages will not be formally legitimist, for the principle of social realism will supplant that of juridical formalism; their environment will not be one of castes but of professional and cultural representatives hierarchically unified; power will be strong, often dictatorial, for the people will instinctively invest men of outstanding merit with the sacred attributes of power. But monarchy cannot be forced on people. They will decide forms of government for themselves, in a real and living way and in accordance with their beliefs. However, this sort of "sovereignty of the people," which in a sense has always existed, cannot be called democracy, and moreover, the question of forms of power is only contingent and secondary.

The principle of work, spiritual and material, will be found at the root of future societies: not, as in Socialism, of work of which the goodness or badness does not matter, but of work considered qualitatively. That was always the Christian idea. The excessive leisure and laziness of the privileged classes of modern history will vanish. Aristocracy will be preserved, but it will gain a more spiritual character, psychological rather than sociological. Life will become more austere, without its modern showiness. A very strong tension will be set up for the human spirit, and a particular sort of monastic life in the world, a kind of new religious order, may emerge. The problem will present itself as a religious one, the santification of work, a problem which has no interest for modern history because it has tried frenziedly to free all men from the "burden" of work: both Capitalism and Socialism have "solved" it by mechanization. Work must be understood as a participation in creation, and great occupational activity combined with a cutting-down of "wants" will characterize the whole of society in this new period of history. It is only thus that impoverished mankind can continue to exist. The centre of gravity will have to be moved from the means of living, in which men to-day are absorbed exclusively, to the last ends of life; this involves a turning to the inner substance of life itself instead of projecting it outwardly, in time and into the future. The notion of "progress" will be discarded as camouflaging the true ends of life: there will be life, there will be creation, there will be turning to God or to Satan—but there will be no progress as the nineteenth century understood it. We must decrease the speed of that ever-moving current which is bearing us on to nothingness, and acquire a taste for eternity. But parallel to all this another force will be at work whose object will be the spread of the power of sham civilization, and that will be the spirit of Antichrist.

It seems to me that women will be very much to the fore in the new middle ages; an exclusively masculine culture was undermined by the war, and in these later most trying years the influence of women has been considerable and their achievements recognized as great. Woman is bound more closely than man to the soul of the world and its primary elemental forces, and it is through her that he reaches communion with them. Masculine culture is too rationalizing, out of touch with the mysteries of universal life: this is corrected through woman. Women are filling a notably important *rôle* in the present religious revival; as in the gospel, they are predestined to be the myrrh-bearers. Day is the time of the exclusive predominance of masculine culture; at night the feminine element receives her rights.

This extended activity of women in the future does not at all mean a development of that "women's emancipation" with which we are familiar, the end and method of which is to reduce woman to the likeness of man by leading her along a masculine road. That is an anti-hierarchical and equalitarian movement which nullifies the original quality of the female nature. The masculine principle must dominate the feminine and not be her slave, as is so often seen nowadays, in France, for example. It is the *eternal feminine* that has so great a future in coming history, not the emancipated woman or the epicene creature.

Naturally she will be closely associated with that crisis of domestic life and the family which is one of the deep causes of world-disturbance today. The hopes of Christianity cannot stop at human reproduction, an element too close to the "malignant endlessness" of mere successive generations. A fundamental problem of life is just this of the transfiguration of human sexual relations, of the enlightening of the feminine element, of the turning of generative energy into creative energy: the natural generation of the old Adam must become the spiritual generation of the new Adam. This means finding the mystical meaning of love, of a transfiguring love that looks not to time but to eternity. Here we cross the frontier of modern history and leave the rational day to enter the dark night of the middle ages. The mysticism of love cannot be treated with the vocabulary of our days.

The popularity of theosophical doctrine, the taste for occultism, and the revival of magic is another symptom of the new middle ages. Physical science herself goes back to her origins in sorcery and we shall soon have a revelation of the magical character of technique. Religion and science are making contact again and the need for a religious "gnosis" becomes apparent. We are re-making the atmosphere of marvel, so foreign to modern history, and so make possible the return of magic, black and white. And there is, too, the renewal of impassioned discussions of the mysteries of the divine life. So we go from an age that was animistic to one that will be spiritual. But the future is doubtful, and I do not believe that we are obliged to look forward to a period of radiance and joy. The illusions of earthly happiness no longer have any hold on us, and the sense of evil becomes stronger and more acute in the middle ages: the powers of wickedness will grow and take on new forms wherewith to plague us in new ways. But freedom of spirit, liberty to choose his path, has been given to man. Christians must will the creation of a Christian society and culture, putting before all things the search for the Kingdom of God and his justice. A very great deal depends on our liberty, that is, on man's creative efforts. Two ways are open. I have a presentiment that an outbreak of the powers of evil is at hand, but I have preferred to outline the possible positive traits of a future society. *We* are men of the middle ages, not only because that is our destiny, the fatality of history, but also because we will it. *You*, you are still men of modern times, because you refuse to choose.

The night is coming and we must take up spiritual

weapons for the fight against evil, we must make more sensitive our power for its discernment, we must build up a new knighthood.

> The flood waxes and bears us on
> to a dark immensity . . .
> there where we sail, all around us
> the flaming abyss.

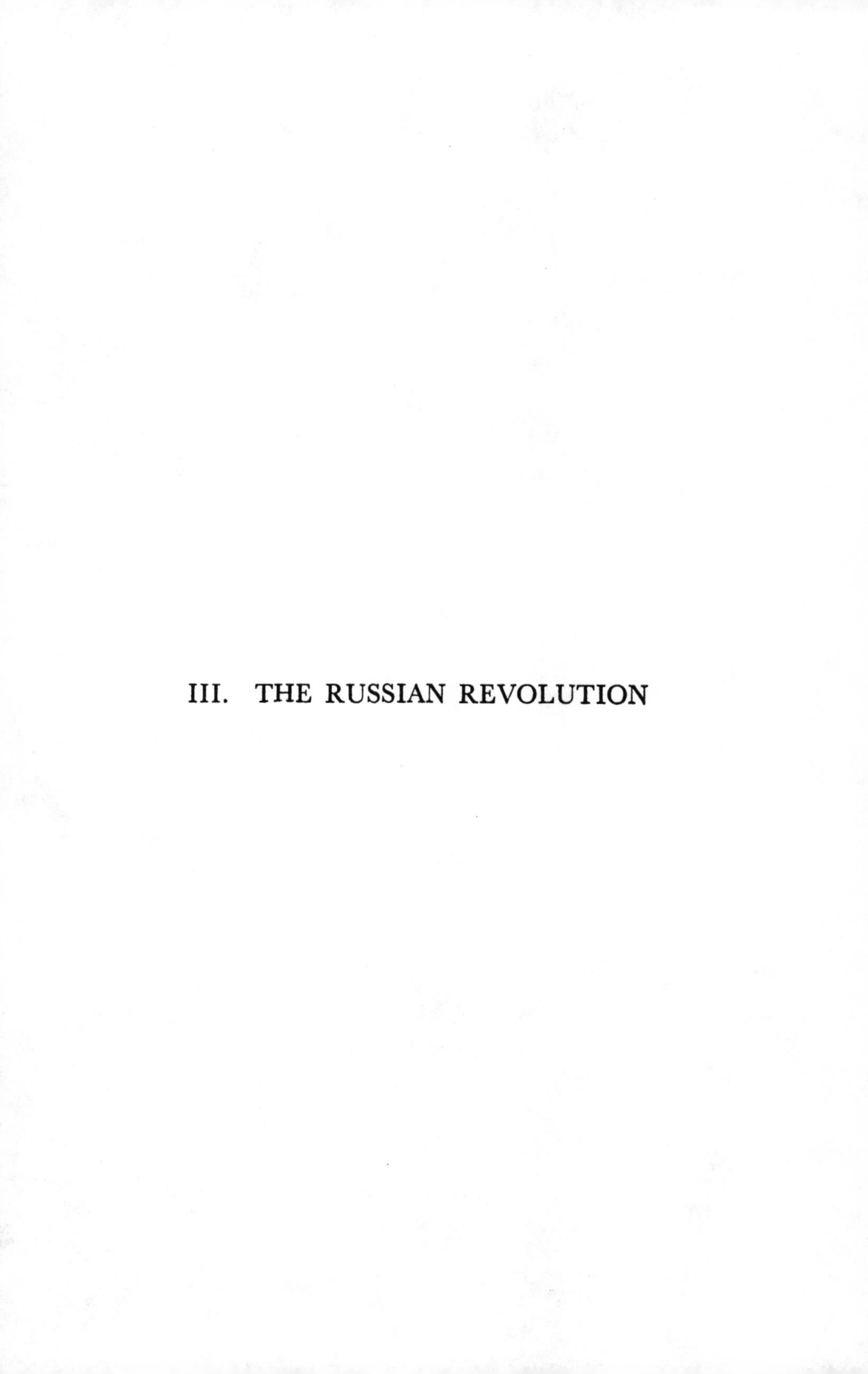

III. THE RUSSIAN REVOLUTION

III. THE RUSSIAN REVOLUTION

I

THERE has been a revolution in Russia. This does not need to be stated, but the recognition of a fact does not imply appreciation of its significance. The Russian revolution is a calamity. So, for that matter, is every revolution; there never has been a good one. But revolutions are permitted by the divine wisdom and so there is a lot to be learned from them.

Revolutions are never fine, harmonious, and happy, and that in Russia is infamous like all the rest of them. Moreover, they are always ineffectual. The French revolution, which is called "great," was itself infamous and a failure. It was no better than the Russian one, no less bloody, no less cruel; it was just as atheistical and as destructive of all that history had hitherto held holy. The Russian revolution is not called "great" and has no moral halo; it is only important. But historians will arise who will idealize it, canonize it, praise it exaggeratedly, make a legend out of it and crown it with a diadem. And then other historians will come along to unmask this myth and overthrow the legend.

The unhappy Russians, who have suffered so cruelly, morally and materially, seem to have forgotten what a revolution always is. It is more agreeable to read about one in history-books than to live during one. Is not the exaggerated indignation against the bolshevists, the attribution of all the crimes exclusively to them, often the result of a certain idealization of revolution, as if people had not got over the illusion that such a thing can be beneficial and grand? Man's memory is very short during a revolutionary period. Many are ambitious to direct the storm, and are furious when they can't do it; they forget that it is no more possible to steer a revolution than to put a brake on it. The bolshevists have not guided the revolution in Russia, but have just been its obedient servants. Most criticisms of it are grounded on the supposition that it need never have happened or else that it could have been carried on prudently and gently but for those dastardly bolshevists—but looked at thus it becomes impossible to catch its true significance and to realize its tragedy interiorly. There is nothing more pitiable than the frequent discussions among Russian *émigrés* of the questions: "Are the happenings in Russia a revolution or only just 'troubles'?" and "Who are responsible?" That is a completely useless and doting way of comforting oneself. In fact, every revolution is a succession of disturbances, a progressive decomposition of an old society and its culture. We must give up our notion of revolution according to ideal and pattern. A revolution is never what it ought to be, for there is no such thing as revolution of strict obligation, it cannot be a bounden duty. It is an affliction on man and an immense disaster. And it behoves us to bear this disaster with dignity, the same dignity with which we should bear an illness or the death of a friend.

There are some who think revolution can be controlled from the ground of pre-revolutionary principles. These people are entirely without a perspective of history and are shutting their eyes to what a revolution is. It is as it were an infectious epidemic of serious disease, and once it is caught it gets hold of the whole body and nothing can stop it taking its course. Temperature will rise till the patient is delirious, and then it will fall below normal. So revolution has to work itself out and get over its violent period before it is checked and overtaken by its contrary, that the antidote may come from the bane itself. The extreme tendencies are bound to win and the more moderate to be repudiated and swamped. Those who inaugurated the revolution or who willed it always perish in it. Such is the law of revolution and, according to the master-mind of Joseph de Maistre, such is the will of Providence, always at work in revolutions according to its mysterious way; God allows revolutions to punish men and nations. Any hope that wiser and more moderate parties, *girondins* or constitutional democrats,* can hold in check and direct the elements of revolution is a piece of silly rationalizing, the most unrealizable of all dreams.

In the Russian revolution the bolshevists were the realists and the constitutional democrats the dreamers. Could anything be more lacking in common sense than the plan they cherished of turning Russia into a democratic country, firmly believing that the people could be persuaded by humanitarian speeches to acknowledge the rights and liberties of men and citizens and that it would be possible by liberal enactments to uproot the fierce instincts of both governors and governed? That would indeed have been an incredible revolution, a negation of all the age-long impulses and traditions of the Russian people. It would have been far more radical than the bolshevist policy, which uses the accepted ways of government and exploits the secular characteristics of the people. The bolshevists were not "maximisers" but "minimisers,"† seeking the line of least resistance, in full agreement with the clamorous desires of soldiers worn out by war and avid for peace, of peasants who coveted the

* A pre-revolutionary Russian political party with a liberal programme.—Tr.

† There is a play on words here in the original Russian. *Bolshevik* means "maximalist"; their socialist opponents were called *menshevik*, "minimalist."—Tr.

lands of their lords, of angry and vindictive wage-earners. The maximizers were those who wanted to carry on the war at all costs, not those who made up their minds to be done with it when it had gone bad inside. Those who fomented the irrational elements of the revolution acted, in a way, more wisely, more in accord with facts, than those who tried to make out of them a theoretical scheme of rational politics. The revolution from its own point of view was right to destroy theoretical and reasoned politics, for such have no organic principle, elemental force, or deep roots. Bolshevism is rationalized lunacy, a mania for the definitive regulation of life, resting on the elemental irrationality of the people. But the rationality of liberal politicians, ready though it is to concede certain rights to irrationality, does not rest on any elemental force whatsoever. Bolshevism was, in an inverted, paradoxical way, in accordance with the "Russian idea," and that is why it has triumphed. It was helped by the fact that the Russians have only a very weak hierarchical feeling, while the tendency to autocratic authority is correspondingly strong; they have not wanted to have anything to do with a constitutional government.

II

When revolution has overtaken a people the unhappy fact must be accepted as though it were the work of divine providence. We can only receive it humbly, like all the other sufferings, misfortunes, and serious trials of life: resisting its temptations to the utmost of our spiritual powers, being faithful to all our sacred things, carrying the torch down into the catacombs, bearing the scourge by the enlightening help of a religious mind, seeing in it the means of satisfaction for our sin; at the same time aiding and co-operating with the vital currents around us, the positive formations thanks to which revolution evolves towards its contrary, towards the creation of something true and good. Morally, it is wrong to suppose that the source of evil is outside oneself, that one is a vessel of holiness running over with virtue. Such a disposition is the best soil for a hateful and cruel fanaticism. It is as wrong to impute every wickedness to Jews, Freemasons, "intellectuals," as it is to blame all crimes on to the *bourgeoisie*, the nobility, and the powers that were. No; the root of evil is in me as well, and I must take my share of the responsibility and the blame. That was true before the revolution and it is true still.

A myriad tiny spiritual and material influences in the interior life of the people prepare the end of the revolution, leading invisibly to an issue. During its course, civil wars cannot be avoided and they call for great heroism and much unselfishness. But civil wars will never end a revolution or undo its tragedy: they belong entirely to its irrational side, they are part of and make worse its work of disaggregation. Warfare between revolutionaries and counter-revolutionaries in arms is generally a contest between the forces of revolution and the forces of *before* the revolution, that is, the very forces at which the revolution is aimed. Real counter-revolution can be effected only by *after*-revolutionary forces—by those developed in the womb of the revolution itself. Counter-revolution is the opening of a new era and it cannot be the work of classes and parties which have been gravely injured and thrown from their places of power precisely by the revolution. It was not the nobles, the *émigrés*, the people scattered by the irresistible torrent of the Revolution, who put an end to the troubles in France: it was Napoleon, "the son of the Revolution." By a sort of pathological process working itself out in the organism, revolution begets within itself the forces which will eventually free it from its own devils. Someone who has "carried it all within himself" (Tiutchev: *On Napoleon*) is most often the one who has to untie all its tangled knots and find the way out: no external force can do it. Bonapartism is a characteristic end to revolution. Oliver Cromwell and Napoleon Bonaparte were men of destiny carrying in their hands the fate of a revolution—and that is what made their mightiness.

Both the experience of history and our own personal moral experience teach us that revolutions can be conquered only by post-revolutionary forces, by elements different from those in power before and during the revolution. Everything pre-revolutionary is only an internal element of the revolution, part of the revolutionary decomposition; "pre-revolutionary" and "revolutionary" are only the same entity seen at different times, and the revolution itself is the consummated dissolution of the old order. There is salvation neither in that which has begun to corrupt nor in that which has corrupted completely, but only in a life newly conceived. The Russian territorial nobility who want their lands back, the old *bourgeoisie* who want their factories and their capital, the old-style "intellectuals" yearning to restore the prestige of their ideas and to put into practice their political programmes of the day before yesterday, none of these can possibly put an end to the revolution in Russia and free the world from its bloody nightmare. Who can, then? The peasants, the new middle-class born of the revolution, the Red Army recovered from its bloodthirsty delirium, the new intellectuals who have gained a deeper spiritual substance and new positive ideas from their tragic experience. Is this good or bad? Neither. It is fate.

There is nothing particularly happy to be looked forward to in post-revolutionary Russia; its devastation is too complete, its demoralization too terrible, the level of culture must necessarily fall very low.

But destiny must be looked in the face. Nobody is bound to have an optimistic outlook on the future: that is not a precept of the Christian religion. The world is moving towards a tragic duality and a struggle between opposed spiritual forces. But it is a matter of immense importance that illusions should be dispelled and man come face to face with positive realities. And it is with revolutions as with everything else in history: they never achieve what they hoped to achieve, and their significance is ignored by those even who took the most active part in them. It remains for us to set our will towards the realization of the truth so admirably expressed by Joseph de Maistre: "A counter-revolution must not be a contrary revolution but the contrary of a revolution."

It is impossible to live by a negative sentiment, by feelings of hatred, anger, and revenge. Russia cannot be saved by these. The revolution has poisoned her with vindictiveness and made her drunk with blood. What will happen if a counter-revolution poisons her with a new vindictiveness and intoxicates her with fresh blood? Things would be worse, not better. The communion of anger and hate is one and indivisible, it unites Communists to extreme Royalists. Life needs positive elements for its principle, the negative can create nothing. Our love must always prevail over our hate; we must love Russia and her people more than we can possibly hate the revolution and the bolshevists. A mighty love for the Russian land and the Russian soul must be at the heart of our politics; that alone may be regarded as a normal spiritual condition. The bolshevist revolution has been begun and carried on by negative sentiments: it is a masterpiece of fury. To direct negative sentiments of equal force against it and to combat it with rage in our hearts is to continue the work of destruction. Yet it must be admitted with sadness that those who have been cruelly hit and hurt by the revolution are too often carried away by negative violent emotions, thereby showing that they have not grasped its spiritual meaning and that they have lived it only in a physical, external sense. Indeed, the great problem, for Russia and for the world, is the finding of a way out of the death-dealing circle of revolutions and reactions, a way leading to a new social order. Only a malignant endlessness of these reactions and revolutions can be seen down the road of purely negative reaction. Blood breeds blood; and the people have been long since made ill with blood. We must free ourselves from the control of these negative reactions. It is our spiritual duty, an obligation on Christians.

The revolution was a dark and bloody reaction against the evil of the old life which preceded it; it was a cruel reaction against a cruel reaction. To read the letters of the last Russian Tsarina to the last Russian Tsar is to understand in the very depths of one's being that the revolution was predestined and ineluctable, that the old regime was definitely condemned, that any return to that past is impossible. This condemnation leaves the personality of those who were martyrs untouched; as men and women they were worth a great deal more than those who rule the country to-day. But there are no such things as restorations. There are sporadic convulsive movements of forces to which revolution has brought final decomposition; and then later on there are new activities taking shape from forces bred by the revolution trying to consolidate their vital gains. It is senseless to want to restore anything that led to a revolution: as well shut oneself up in a magic circle. It is no good looking for a way out in a lateral movement to right and left; it can only be found vertically, in height and depth. The counter-revolution of ideas must be headed towards the making of a *new* life, wherein past and future shall be one in eternity, and at the same time be rigidly set against all forms of reaction. The revolution has destroyed every kind of freedom in Russia, and the counter-revolution must give it back to her: freedom to breathe, to think, to move about, to stop at home, to live a spiritual life. This may sound paradoxical—it is meant to be understood in all its wideness and fullness.

III

The revolution must not be considered only externally, as though one saw in it simply an empirical fact without any relation to *my* spiritual life and to *my* destiny. If a man keeps up that attitude he will choke himself with impotent anger. The revolution did not take place only outside and beyond me, an event having no common measure with my own life and so without any meaning for me; it was also as it were an interior happening within me. Bolshevism has been embodied in Russia and triumphed there because *I* am what I *am*, because there was no real spiritual power in me, none of the strength of faith that can move mountains; it is my sin, and an affliction that is visited on me. The suffering that it has caused me is a satisfaction for my failure and for my iniquity, for our common failure and our common iniquity: all are responsible for all. This way of living and of understanding a revolution is the only one which religion can inspire, the only one that brings any light to the soul. The Russian revolution is the destiny of the Russian people—and my destiny; the ransom and reparation due from the people—and from me.

Would that those of "the right" would give up their self-satisfied and unworthy air of injured innocence! Their offences are grave and they must submit to a heavy penance. The revolution must be borne with dignity and moral courage to the bitter end, as a burden sent from God; those who so bear will find salvation in it. Those who see in Bolshevism only the external violence of a band of robbers preying on the people have formed a superficial and wrong conception. The historical destinies of peoples cannot be looked at like that: it is the point of view of small-minded men who have suffered or of combatants blinded by the rage of battle. The bolshevists are not brigands who have fallen on Russia in the highway of her history and bound her hand and foot: their victory is not at all a matter of chance. Bolshevism is a much deeper phenomenon, more terrible and more frightening; it is inherent in the Russian people, a serious moral disease, their organic defect. But it is not an independent ontological reality, it has no being of itself; it is a reflection of the tendency to wickedness that there is in all of us, an hallucination of the diseased popular mind. Bolshevism corresponds to the moral condition of us Russians and displays outwardly our inward crises, our loss of faith, our religion in danger, the hideous weakening of our moral life.

Soviet power is not democratic and was not established by any constituent assembly. But has anybody ever seen formalities create power? It is always constituted by might; and the power of the Soviets seemed the only conceivable one in Russia at the moment of her supreme weakness, when the war collapsed because she had no more strength to wage it, when moral downfall, economic disaster, and the failure of all her spiritual foundations were upon her. Bolshevist power at that time appeared as a national power, though in a sense in no wise flattering to it; nevertheless, this must be recognized if the revolution is to be understood. No other power could be created in the moral and historical atmosphere that obtained when the revolt was let loose: the people found themselves in a false position and made a false power. Bolshevism alone was able to organize after a fashion and curb the demoniac element whose fetters it had broken. The true principle of the authority of power was lost. The pitiable and helpless part played by the Provisional Government showed that power could not be organized on humanitarian lines, neither the liberal democratic idea nor the spirit of a moderate socialism could be relied on. As for the monarchical principle, it had been degraded and scorned for a century; now it crumpled up. It still existed only because it was sanctioned by the religious beliefs of the people. The authority of power always does rest on religious beliefs; when those beliefs are extinguished authority is shaken and falls. That is what happened in Russia. Popular religion underwent a change; "enlightenment"—and in Russia enlightenment always takes nihilistic forms—was gaining influence among the people. Only the bolshevists were able to organize a power which was in sympathy with the new beliefs and with the savage war-element.

When moral enthusiasm for the war waned it was transmuted into an orgy of slaughter, a fight of all against all. There was then room only for a dictatorship of brutality and blood. All the solid elements, come forward to preserve the cultured caste, were swamped, for their over-refined culture had been able to subsist only by virtue of the monarchy which prevented popular ignorance from overflowing. Russia was a vast shadowy empire of peasants (*muzhiks*), among whom classes were but weakly developed; an educated caste very insignificant numerically; and a tsar, master of the empire, who alone stood in the way of the people devouring the *élite*. Granted that the imperial authority often persecuted and terrorized this *élite*, still it also made its existence possible and so up to a point provided for a hierarchy of quality in Russian life. The fall of the imperial power brought on a "simplifying fusion": all qualitative differences were destroyed, the whole structure of society was broken up, overrun by the dark tide of soldiers and peasants; the cultured *élite*, having no roots in a more solid social class, was thrown into the seething pit. In such conditions the monarchical power could be replaced only by the power of the Soviets: one more cultured could not have existed, for it would have been completely cut off from the condition and mood of the people. We witnessed a horrible degradation of life, manners became brutalized, the muzhiko-military era had begun.

God, if I may dare say so, transferred authority to the bolshevists for the punishment of the people, and this is why their power possesses a mysterious strength, which the bolshevists themselves cannot understand. Is it not remarkable that in the Russian revolution there have been no contests between opponents, no activity of parties? This differentiates it profoundly from the French Revolution: when a *montagnard* or a *girondin* went to the guillotine it was as a citizen incidentally beaten in the scuffle. But there was no civic sentiment in the Russian revolution: we are taken away to be shot with a feeling in our heart of submission to a controlling and sinister force.

There was hardly any culture in Russia except that of the nobles. It no longer exists. The nobility are dispossessed and dispersed. And it must be said that they contributed a great deal to their own downfall: they were degenerate and had lost all sense of their responsibility towards their position. Their form of culture—which was also supreme in other classes, the bourgeois and the intellectual—has given place to the muzhiko-military and proletarian style. That power, brutal and ferocious in its methods, has declared war on all quality in favour of quantity, and only the Soviet authority, hostile to all fine culture, is able to govern a country branded with such a mark. The first place is held by a new category of vigorous men, graduated in the school of war, harsh, grasping and cruel; they apply all the methods of war to civil government, which means that they carry on the war, with other objects, within the nation itself. Soviet power is a military power, exercised in the manner of conquerors. But that does not at all mean that these conquerors are as it were foreigners to the people; they were proclaimed by the people themselves in the time of their dissolution and sanguinary corruption. The bolshevists have made real the popular dream of a "black redistribution" of the land, and they are admirably in accord with the ideals of Russian nihilism. It is a very unpopular power and no one is in sympathy with it, but it may well seem to be the only possible one where a people has deserved it; and the Russians in the midst of a bankrupt war and a corrupt revolution deserved nothing else.

This is not at all equivalent to saying that the Russian people is bolshevist. The catastrophe occurred in the very depths of Russian society, underneath its cultural layer; it occurred within the people's soul. The people, indeed, have never been able to acquiesce in the educated classes or the landed gentry, not only from a social but from a religious point of view as well. The effective distance between the upper and the lower class had always been so great among us that there was nothing like it in any other country of the West. The people did not accept the war, and later they did not accept a democratic and humanitarian authority.

When considering the revolution and possible ways of salvation for Russia there is a danger of overlooking the moral condition of the Russians, the state of their belief or unbelief. Everything is settled inwardly, and not outwardly. Now no one is bound to bless popular beliefs and burn incense before the will of the people if those beliefs and that will seem to him worthless. I myself resolutely do not accept the principle of the sovereignty of the people. But it is senseless to ignore their moral state. Power by its very nature is not democratic, but it ought to be popular. When all is said and done, everything is decided by their religious beliefs: it is certainly they that determined the existence of absolute monarchy. And if those beliefs are misleading and worthless it is my first duty to devote my abilities to an attempt to lead my countrymen towards beliefs that are true and good. The truth that spirit and morality must always take precedence of politics needs to be recognized more than ever nowadays. *The Russian question is above all a spiritual question.* There can be no salvation for her apart from a spiritual re-birth; a materialistic contest for power can only aggravate the evil and intensify her decomposition. It is infinitely tragic that those who conduct an active campaign against Communism and the revolution are not moved by any great idea that can be opposed to them. A serious movement against Bolshevism is equally impossible in western Europe, for there too is no consciousness of any truth in whose name a crusade could be proclaimed. The present state of affairs is comparable to that of the third century, when Christianity saved the world spiritually from ruin and complete disintegration. Then, barbarism penetrated a tottering and senile culture; now, the aristocratic foundations of our culture are rocking and an assimilation of a barbarian element is again called for, a new light in the darkness.

Bolshevism cannot be disposed of by a well-organized army, however large. That would only increase the disorder and confirm that abnormal and dangerous condition in which power is in the hands of soldiers and so made a merely external force. That is how the Roman empire perished. Bolshevism must first of all be overcome from within, spiritually, and only afterwards by politics. A new spiritual principle for the organization of authority and culture must be found. The military principle may easily become dangerous and the present situation in Europe strengthens the need to avoid its supremacy. Even apart from Bolshevism a certain militarism threatens to brutalize her life and culture, her politics are rooted in brute force and falsehood, she also has suffered a horrible degradation. This is borne out by the evidence of so important a reaction as Fascism. Contrary to the general opinion, this also has been a revolution, the work of young men trained in the school of war, full of vigour and hungering to play a leading part in life. There is considerable psychological likeness between them and the young men of the Soviets, but fascist energy is used in a different direction, and not destructively but creatively. This is an age of Caesarism, and therein is the chief importance of men of the type of Mussolini, the only person of originality among contemporary European statesmen; he knew how to curb the strong and warlike impulses of the younger generation and direct them to the service of the nation, at the same time giving scope and outlet for their energy.

I am nothing of a pacifist, but there are times when it is needful to stand out against the attempt to submit historical destinies exclusively to military force. Russia perished through the transformation of her people into an army; the army killed the State. Salvation can be found only in a better principle. But capitalist militarism is itself destroyed, after it has abolished war in its old and more noble sense. It is the fatality of war to develop into revolution, and it is this type of revolutionary war that prevails in the world to-day, while the latest technical inventions threaten the existence of mankind itself. No; the problem of Bolshevism is not a matter of mechanics to be solved by arms: it is primarily interior and moral. The idea of ridding Russia of the bolshevists by machine-guns and bombing-planes, as if they were a band of brigands oppressing the people, is altogether too extrinsic and superficial. The great majority of Russians loathe the bolshevists, yet they find themselves in a state of bolshevism and sheer falsehood. That is a paradox that must be carefully studied and understood. They must be freed from that state of bolshevism, overcome the bolshevism that is in their own hearts. Am I then advocating a passive attitude in opposition to the activity preached by those who want to liquidate the Russian tragedy by force of arms? During the decline of the Roman power and of the whole world of antiquity Diocletian expended a great deal of energy in his efforts to consolidate the empire. But was St. Augustine less active than that emperor? Does he not hold a more important place in the history of the world?

We need works like those of St. Augustine more than anything else. We want faith, we want ideas. Those who can recreate faith will save the societies that are now perishing. Groups of believers are the web on which the new material of society will be woven, they will hold the social threads together when the old states finally collapse—and they are collapsing, modern history is coming to an end. We are approaching, I say it again, an epoch analogous to the beginning of the middle ages. The reactionaries, the people who are behind the times, are all those who want to carry on with the help of the principles of modern history, to maintain the ideas of the nineteenth century, whether those ideas are called Democracy, Humanitarian Socialism, or what not. The revolution which is slowly taking place in Europe may have the effect of a reaction—as, for example, in the case of Fascism in Italy. But it is in reality directed against the foundations of modern history, against an unsubstantial liberalism, against individualism, against juridical formalism.

IV

It is most useful to recall nowadays the ideas about revolution set forth by Joseph de Maistre in that magnificent work *Considérations sur la France;* he was the first to define something essential in the nature of all revolution; it is satanic. Revolutionaries are only independent agents in appearance; in reality they are tools of a force, a superior force, of which they know nothing. But revolutions are providential as well as satanic: they are visited on the people for their sins, a means of expiation.

Joseph de Maistre was not a man of the old pre-revolutionary regime: he understood the special grandeur of a revolution and appreciated its quality of inevitability. He was the greatest thinker of the reaction at the beginning of the nineteenth century, chief of the theocrats, a royalist who believed that it was the *jacobins* who were working for the good of France whereas the *émigrés* desired her dismemberment and defeat. He looked on counter-revolution by force as a definite evil, and was content to wait patiently until an organic ground should be ready for a re-establishment of the monarchy. Maistre was not fond of the *émigrés*; he judged their activities severely, as unpatriotic and against the true interest of the nation.

"The *émigrés*," he says, "are nothing and cannot do anything. . . . One of the laws of the French revolution is that when the *émigrés* attack it they only do harm and they have no part or lot in anything it achieves.

"Everything they have undertaken has failed and has even turned against them. Not only do their schemes fail but they are so characterized by weakness and insignificance that their authors have come to be regarded merely as men who obstinately defend a lost cause.

They ought to give up wasting their time on external activities; perhaps it is desirable that they should never be seen even in a threatening attitude. . . . The *émigrés* can do nothing; I will even add that they *are* nothing."

Maistre, who had such a forbidding reputation, advocated a peaceful and bloodless, even a gentle counter-revolution; he was a declared opponent of revenge. With great discernment he saw that the spokesmen of after-, that is, counter-revolutionary justice must not be those who had been damaged by the revolution, because they would proceed by way of reprisals: "To have to judge the murderer of his father, of his relatives, of a friend, or even the taker of one's property, is the most difficult thing that can happen to a sensitive man. But that is exactly the situation in a counter-revolution as commonly understood: by the nature of the case the judges would almost all belong to the injured class, and justice, even when administered fairly and by way of legal punishment, would have the appearance of revenge."

Those supremely noble words may well be repeated to-day when a desire of revenge is so easily mistaken for an impartial judgement.

Maistre was further of the opinion that the people must eat the bitter fruit of the revolution till they were satiated and sick with it; in other words, that the revolution should devour itself, and he saw a providential justice in the fact that the revolutionaries exterminated one another. People never get what they aim at, and if the French revolution was to have any positive value it would not be that which the revolutionaries themselves tried to give to it. One of the *positive* results of that revolution was Joseph de Maistre himself. The Catholic and Romantic movements of the early nineteenth century became possible only in consequence of the revolution, they were a positive achievement of the revolution. In the same way a consequent deeper conception of religion and spiritual awakening will be seen in Russia; Christianity will begin a new life with the Church freed from the shackles of the State. But, though the judgements of Joseph de Maistre were made with a fine detachment and have still great worth, it must be remembered that the "emigration" caused by the Russian revolution is dissimilar from that of the French. It is made up of very varied elements which include one of very deep culture, and it can have great positive influence in the cultural order if only it can overcome the specifically *émigré* mentality; it has much to suffer, and there are many young people capable of heroism and real selflessness. The objects of the Russian emigration are above all spiritual and not at all political, but it has not yet found the ideas that are to inspire it. A return to the political forms which till recently governed life and intellect cannot be called an "idea"; all past political forms, whether monarchical or democratic, have had their day and are worthless by themselves.

V

The Russian revolution has turned out just as Dostoievsky foresaw it. With prophetic vision he drew its portrait and told us the dialectic of its ideas; he understood that Socialism in Russia was a religious matter, a question of atheism, and that the real concern of the pre-revolutionary intellectuals was not politics but the salvation of mankind without the help of God. If you want to understand the meaning of the revolution you must make these intuitions of Dostoievsky your own. Its causes were numberless and several of them jump to the eye, among them the ghastly war, which Russia was able to bear neither morally nor materially, the underdevelopment of a sense of law among the Russians, their lack of real culture, the defective agrarian organization among the peasants, the hold of false ideas over the intellectuals. But the deeper meaning of the revolution is not to be sought in these directions but rather in its primary spiritual phenomenon. The science of history tells us of the causes which lead to events, but the philosophy of history is concerned with discovery of the essential spiritual phenomena which must be examined if the meaning of historical developments is to be understood. For modern history we find this phenomenon in Humanism and its internal dialectic; this was at the bottom of the French Revolution, though there were of course numerous specific causes as well. And I maintain that the revolution in Russia, an unloosing of elemental forces, half-asiatic, half-barbarian, in the midst of a failing war, had as its principle a religious fact in consonance with the Russian religious nature. The Russians are incapable of bringing forth a "happy-medium" humanitarian kingdom, they do not want a juridical state as understood by Europeans. They are spiritually a non-political people who aspire only to the highest point of history, the actualization of the Kingdom of God; they tend either to this Kingdom, to brotherhood in Christ, or to comradeship in Antichrist, the kingdom of the prince of this world.

The Russians have always been informed by a spirit of detachment from the world quite unknown to western peoples; it is their main characteristic. They have never felt themselves tied and bound to earthly things, to property, family, the State, to their rights, to an external way of life; and in so far as they were attached to these things it was through their sins, and their sins were not less but graver than those of European peoples. As a people they are probably less simply well-behaved, less "decent," than Westerners. But whereas the very virtues of these last tie them down to earth and their material possessions thereon, the Russian virtues cut the people off from earth and turn their hearts to Heaven, and the Orthodox religion directs them into the same path. To a man of western Europe property is sacred and he will not let himself be robbed without a forcible defence, and he holds a system of ideas that justifies that attitude. Though the passions of greed and avarice belong no less to his nature, a Russian does not look on his property as sacred, he has no philosophical justification for having temporal possessions at all, and he believes in his heart that it would be better for him to be a monk or a wandering pilgrim. The ease with which private property has been abolished in Russia is due as well to this national spirit of detachment from earthly goods as to the weakness of their idea of law and to the absence of certain "solid" qualities which flourish among the middle classes: what is a virtue in the eyes of a European bourgeois may well seem sin to a native of Russia where even landed proprietors did not have an absolute conviction that they had a just title to the lands which they held. A. S. Khomiakov* was no isolated example when he claimed to occupy his lands only by virtue of a mandate from the people in order that they might be properly worked. The merchant likewise was persuaded that he made his profits by very doubtful means and that sooner or later he would have to do penance for them. The Christianity of the Orthodox Church emphasizes

* Slavophil writer and lay theologian, 1804-1860. He is considered to be the founder of a purely Russian school of theological thought.—Tr.

the idea of duty rather than that of legal right; we do not fulfil these duties, for we are sinners, but neither do we regard law as an end in itself. Bourgeois ideology has never been valid for us or acted on our hearts, we have never accepted its clearly idealistic basis of rights. Radically, practically all of us looked on the bourgeois regime as sinful: not only the revolutionary Socialists but also the slavophils, the believers, all the men of letters, and even the bourgeois themselves, who always suffered moral humiliation from their status.

It is no good opposing the European bourgeois to the Russian communist; the spiritual formation of the Russian people prevents any victory over Communism by a bourgeois regime in the name of its own ideas. Khomiakov and Leontiev,* Dostoievsky and Leo Tolstoy, Vladimir Soloviev and Nicholas Fedorov† abolished the bourgeois spirit and system not less than did the Socialists and Communists. That is the Russia "idea" and vocation, and patriots should keep it in mind. The Russian Christian holds that, before God, the European bourgeois is no better than the Russian communist, and no Russian wants the one to supplant the other: he refuses to substitute for communist wickedness those bourgeois

* A writer of the last century who in theory advocated extreme conservatism and aristocracy. He began his career in diplomacy and died a monk of the Troitza monastery near Moscow in 1891.—TR.

† Librarian in a Moscow public library. He was well known as an original thinker and ascete. Author of the amazing *Philosophy of the Common Work*.—TR.

virtues whose goodness he denies; a secular culture, a well-established and thoroughly respectable civilization, do not tempt him. That is why Socialism has with us taken on a sacred character and why we now have a pseudo-church and a pseudo-theocracy. We have always been at enmity in spirit with the rule of the bourgeois nineteenth-century civilization; we do not like it and see in it a degradation of the soul. The revolutionary Herzen* and the reactionary Leontiev were in entire agreement on this point. Nor is it any good to think of teaching to Russians German or French patriotism, the nationalism of western Europe; Russian nationalists and patriots in this sense seem completely foreign to the soul of their race. All these things must be taken into account if our revolution is to be understood. And we have not adopted an ideology of the State any more than of the bourgeois; Katkov† was not one of our characteristic thinkers. Our moral spirit cannot accept the supremacy of the state-idea, it remains always subordinate and often disappears altogether: a certain anarchism is proper to us. That the people of Russia tend always towards the Kingdom of God

* A political writer of revolutionary tendencies, born in 1812. Emigrated in 1847 and never returned to Russia. From London he published his paper *Kolokol*, which had great influence in Russian liberal circles of the time. Died in 1870.—Tr.

† Journalist and writer of extreme conservative views, 1818-1887. His paper, the *Moskovskia Vedomosti*, had much and often bad influence upon Russian politics.—Tr.

accounts for their virtues—and for many of their vices as well. For Paradise eludes us. And yet there is a duty of obedience to the world that man has to shoulder on earth; it exists in relation to historical development and this duty is often forgotten by Russians. That is the chief reason why our hideous revolution must be called national. Though the soul of the Russian man reaches out to the Kingdom of God he easily yields to temptation, he is deceived by shams and illusions, he succumbs before the powers of darkness, and the reign of falsehood and deceit is now established in his land. There is something of another world, from "beyond," about the bolshevists. That, I think, is what makes them so sinister. Currents as it were of preternatural energy emanate from the most ordinary among them. Behind every bolshevist there is a collective sorcery which bewitches the people into a magic sleep, encloses them in a charmed circle. Russia must be exorcized. That is the capital task.

VI

The Russian revolution must be experienced in the depths of the soul in order that there shall be a *katharsis*, an interior cleansing. It cannot be lived spiritually by the covetous who want their lost possessions back, by those whose hearts are angry, who clamour for punishment: that is a worldly way to receive its sufferings, indicative of a bourgeois attitude. Nor is the revolution lived in spirit by him who accommodates himself to it and does not guard the freedom of his interior being, and still less by him who dreams, without the least awareness of his own sin, of a restoration of the pre-revolutionary social life. Sincere repentance will allow these sufferings to be undergone only in a spiritual sense. New life begins with the mystery, the sacrament, of penance; only that can free us from the tyranny of a dark past, from oppression by spectres and ghosts. The psychology of Christian repentance is diametrically opposed not only to the psychology of the revolution but also to that of the restoration, which is always vindictive and angered. Desire for revenge and for the restoration of the old life with all its sinfulness is not compatible with penitence, which strains towards a new life: such wishes belong to impenitent offenders.

To experience the revolution in spirit and in one's being is to gauge the importance and depth of this crisis for Russia and for the world. It will not do to give an impression of thinking that nothing exceptionally serious has happened, that it is only a series of outrages, infamies and scandals which can easily be stopped by the police and the military. What can be more pitiable than to see those who have been thrown down from the highest places in society console themselves in this way, by denying the very fact of the revolution and referring to it as "troubles" or "outbreaks of violence"? I am convinced that there has been a revolution in Russia—and that there is a revolution going on in the world analogous to the collapse of the world of antiquity. I am convinced that to advocate a return to the pre-war situation is to declare oneself blind to all that is happening and to evince a judgement unequipped with historical perspective; it is to want to restore outworn and crumbling principles whose decay has already bred frightful carnage and revolution; it is to grasp at a life that is a life of injustice and iniquity. Neither in Russia nor in Europe can we return to that life, nor ought we to be able to: if we could, the miseries and sufferings of our day would be without meaning and justification. This desire to go back to a near past is precisely what is blameworthy and dangerous in the reactionaries. Truly, the revolution has not made a new and better life, it only shows the dissolution of the sinful old ways; but the spiritual experience which we should gain from it can lead us towards a new life that *will* be better. Every right-minded man should be able to see that, whether his view of the immediate future be optimistic or pessimistic. And the new life will be before all a spiritual life. The watchword for each one is: Do what I can, come what may. There is no going back to the old liberalism of the intellectuals, to popular policies, to socialism, any more than to the former monarchy and the life of its nobility.

The Russia of lords and masters is no more, and nothing that was temporal or bad in it can be revived: but what was good and eternal cannot see corruption and it must form a part of all new life. There is an eternal element in aristocracy and the world cannot live without it, but the social importance which our nobility, considered as a class and caste, had in the past will never be again; desire for it can produce only bitterness and hate. No more will the bourgeoisie ever recover its position, for their system of ideas has been turned upside down interiorly. The revolution is not in the interest of the lower classes only but of all in so far as people give up saying "thou"* in favour of "you." Herein is an irrevocable disturbance in our social usages: the old attitude of "the lord" towards "the people" is made impossible. Probably the change from "thou" to "you" will remain the supreme achievement of the revolution so far as manners and customs are concerned. But there would have to be a greater revolution still before the people of the whole world would come to *tutoyer* one another. And it is not external revolutions that bring about such a result: the French Revolution failed to achieve it, despite all its efforts.

*It was the custom in Russia to use the second person singular when addressing the lower class, a custom which was often bitterly resented.—Tr.

Henceforward aristocracy in Russia will not be confined to nobility of birth, the rigid skeleton of social classes has been broken up. This was easy, for our social classes were never a really vigorous institution, but it must be realized that all classes are in fact abolished, with the sole exception of the peasants: nobility and bourgeoisie no longer exist as such, and the communists did away with the "working class" as they went along.* Apart from the peasants there is only the bureaucracy of the soviets and the depressed intellectuals, so it is difficult to see on what elements a restoration could rely. At the same time a new grade has been formed, of an anthropological rather than a social type. The biologically fittest have combined and are found in occupation of all the best positions. I know these young men, in sweaters, clean-shaven and with cropped hair, with a soldierly bearing, very energetic, sensible, determined to get power and watching for a chance to slip into a place in the front ranks, and, generally, very self-assertive and off-hand. They are to be met with everywhere, they control everything. You see them riding about in cars, running down men and things, they have the best jobs in Soviet administrations, they shoot men down and make their careers out of the

* There have been developments in the past ten years. There is now a regular class-system in Russia, but on the other hand the peasants as a class have ceased to exist. Stalin was too strong for them and the "anthropological type" is representative of Russia today.—Tr.

revolution. These young men, who outwardly are very unlike the old type of revolutionary and are indeed completely opposed to it, are either communist or adapt themselves to Communism and take on a soviet flavour. They esteem themselves the masters of life and makers of the Russia of the future. And it is indeed thanks to them that the bolshevists are victorious, and the *Tche-ka** is carried on by their efforts. The older generation, the intellectual revolutionaries, dread this new type, scenting a danger to the communist idea; but they have to reckon with it. It forms a new bourgeoisie, but it is not a social class. It is above all an anthropological phenomenon.

The expression on the face of Russia is altered, there has been a change in the people that makes them unrecognizable. We never used to see people like that. This new young man is not in fact a Russian type but an international type. A taste for force and power has arisen in Russia: it is a bourgeois taste that we did not have before, only the bourgeois elements wanted to hatch it and now they are able to stand by and cheer. The war is responsible, for it is there that these young men were formed. Their children and grandchildren will grow into a solid bourgeois type and be quite definitely the backbone

* An abbreviation of *Tchresvytchaynaia Kommissia*: Extraordinary Commission for the Suppression of Counter-revolution; renamed in 1922 as G.P.U.—*Gesudarstvennoe Politicheskoe Upravlenie*: State Political Department.—Tr.

of society. These gentlemen will reach the first places, pushed into them by the *Tche-ka* after hundreds of people have been shot; but no spilling of blood will satisfy their greed for life and power. The most sinister figure in Russia is not the old communist, who is doomed to disappear, but this new young man by whom the soul of his country and the vocation of its people can be given over to damnation. He is capable of upsetting Communism and turning it into Fascism overnight. But that would be no cause for rejoicing. The essential thing is not in those outward forms of life called Communism and Sovietism but in the inward changes that Russia is undergoing; the really terrible fact is that in the course of a communist revolution she is *becoming a bourgeois country for the first time.* Men clever in the things of this world, unscrupulous and full of vigour, have broken in and proclaimed their right to be the masters of life: they do not share the Russian longing for the heavenly Jerusalem. The Russia of the tsars, nobles, peasants, monks, pilgrims, and intellectuals was never a middle-class realm of the *tiers-état.* That which Leontiev feared so frantically has now come to pass, and it is that that has to be considered far more carefully than how to overturn the Soviet power. Our *émigrés* do not sufficiently grasp that the problem of Russia is not a matter of a handful of bolshevists who can be driven from power, but of an enormous body of men of a new kind who have gained ascendency over Russian life and whom it will not be at all easy to drive out.

The communist revolution is primarily a materialization of Russian life, paradoxically joined to a disincarnation of historical formations. Communism is a warfare against the spirit and the good life and its moral consequences are even more terrifying than those political, juridical, and economic, for they will last much longer. The country is going through a period of demoralization comparable to that of the French *Directoire*, but this demoralization and materialization must not be blamed wholly on the communists; it is a far wider phenomenon. The Russians are used to serfdom, they no longer have the same need of liberty, and they have bartered freedom of spirit for material goods. Envy, that black passion, has become the determining force in the world and it is difficult to stay the progress of its development.

Our cultural tradition is broken and we are faced by a distressing lowering of the level of culture and its value. The greater part of Russia is becoming a realm of "civilized" peasants. The new bourgeoisie (by which I do not mean an industrial and banking class but the victorious anthropological social type) calls for a civilization founded on technique but feels no need for any culture that is higher and therefore aristocratic. It is unavoidable that barbarization should be lying in wait for us—we can comfort ourselves with the reflection that, after the war, barbarization to a certain extent had to overtake, and is overtaking, the whole of Europe. The revolution has broken not only the Russian nobility but also the intellectuals in the old sense of the term. For a hundred years they dreamed of and worked for a revolution—and now it has put an end to them. One party of them came to power and the rest have been thrown overboard. The revolution has stripped bare the mistakes in the ideology by which they lived. New intellectual groups will be formed but the level of their culture will be much lower, they will be marked by no highly spiritual tendencies. Even the intellectuals of the period of Tshernyshevsky* were notably less cultured than those of the time of Tshaadaev,† Khomiakov, and Herzen. When the Russian peasant wants to organize his life he will have no need of revolutionary socialists or constitutional democrats or anybody else—he will do it himself.

The old great Russia was full of deep contrasts and extreme oppositions, but nevertheless could be seen as a unity; it was one and the same Russia,

* A writer of the sixties-seventies with socialist tendencies. One of the fathers of Russian nihilism.—Tr.

† A deep and original thinker (1794-1856) who was in many ways the precursor of Soloviev. His works were published by Father J. Gagarin, S.J., in Paris in 1862.—Tr.

from the summits of her culture down to the darkest depths among the masses, that we could feel in the works of her great writers. Apparently this will no more be so; it looks as if there is to be a division into two realms. From the point of view of quality, the eternal Russia of the spirit, destined to say her word at the end of history, will continue to live; but from the point of view of quantity it is probably the Russia of an atheist civilization that will be in the ascendent. Indeed, an analogous division will be manifest throughout the world and, according to all appearances, the enemies of the spirit of Christ will prevail. All our energies must be directed towards the triumph of the eternal Russia, of "quality," and those efforts will not be fruitless for the spiritual ordering of the world.

The psychology of the former revolutionary intellectuals is now transplanted to the counter-revolutionaries among the *émigrés*, and sentiments once roused by the absolute monarchy are directed against Bolshevism, which among them takes the place of the monarchy. In the same way, whereas formerly true life was to begin with the fall of the Throne, now it is to begin with the fall of the Soviets: when the whole of life is put in its outward appearance all hopes rest on political *coups d'état*, which by their nature do not interest man in his inward aspect. Faced by the bolshevist revolution, the counter-revolutionary intellectuals retain the psychology of the old liberals and radicals. But there is nothing more futile in these days than liberalism and radicalism of that sort. It is useful to recall the truths expressed in the "Landmarks,"* which remain valid when applied to Bolshevism: life must, before everything else, be looked at interiorly, spiritually (and not exteriorly or politically as both revolutionaries and counter-revolutionaries do), and lived with spiritual striving and moral discipline. It is wrong to suppose that political forms are in themselves of any efficacy; only the spirit is health-giving, and it creates new forms of its own. New wine must be put into new bottles. Legitimism, whether it be monarchical or democratic, is a dead idea in catastrophic periods of history. For the time we live in, monarchy, besides having to be forced on the people, cannot be an object within the sphere of reality, even for monarchists.

The revolution has inflicted very grave wounds on Russia and they will not easily be healed. But in a sense it must also have positive results, in so far as it will help the work of regenerating the Church and religious life. Revolution always throws light on the real religious conditions of a people. Much unreality and hypocrisy had accumulated in the Russian Orthodox Church; greed of gain and an exterior attitude to life was far too common; there

* *Landmarks on the Road* (*Viekhi*), a collection of essays by several Russian writers, published in 1909, to which M. Berdyaev contributed. —Tr.

was an authoritarianism in morals, familiar to hardened Orthodox, that had to be broken down. The piety of the nobles and the governing class in general was deficient in depth; Christianity was not taken seriously enough. The religion of the Sadducees has always a political cast and the clouds of this life are allowed to obscure the horizon of eternity. There were signs of rigidity in the life of the Church. The revolution has cleared this atmosphere of falsehood and sweetened the soil in which the plant of religion can grow; there is now no point in straining to appear orthodox, no material gain to expect from the Church, no place or function for "political piety."

The character of revolution is always anti-religious and anti-Christian; it persecutes and its persecutions are hateful. But persecution has never been any danger to the Christian life, and is worth far more to the Church than protection by force, for it actually strengthens and spreads true religious life. Christianity is the religion of Truth crucified. By the persecution in our revolution the Church will lose in numbers but she will gain in quality. Christianity calls for powers of selflessness and sacrifice in her faithful, and this capacity for self-surrender has been manifest in Russia. The best of her priests are faithful to their holy calling, they have bravely defended the Faith and equally bravely stood up to be shot. Christians have again shown that they know how to die. The Orthodox Church is humbled and brought low from the outside, but within she is enlarged and lifted up in glory: she has her martyrs. And she has proved that her organic unity, her inward light and mystical foundations, are kept intact even when official ecclesiastical direction and outward forms are overturned and in confusion. Religious concepts and the religious sense are indubitably being strengthened and deepened in Russia; the people live in an atmosphere of religious tension after undergoing so bitter afflictions. The hardness and seriousness of life, the closeness of death, the collapse of all material illusions and the loss of those earthly things which enslave the human spirit, all call them to God and the life of the soul.

The intellectuals, who for a century were hostile to the Faith and preached the atheism which ended in the revolution, are beginning to turn to religion. This is something new. And in Russia itself this movement has no taint of hoped-for gain, it is not associated with any plan for political restoration or hope for a return of the lost pleasures of the past: the Russians have gone through a real spiritual experience which has modified their estimation of temporal possessions. But it must be added with regret that the hierarchs and faithful of the Russian Orthodox Church in exile in the West sometimes submit to the oppressive influence of right-wing political parties, thus reproducing the old relations between Church and State on a small scale. A "practical" and political attitude towards the Church will not allow a renaissance either of religion or of Russia, and the Church cannot be bound to any set political form whatsoever. Only an attitude of spiritual disinterestedness towards the Church, eagerness for sacrifice, and renouncement of temporal privileges can forward the religious revival and the salvation of our country. The hour both of the Sadducees and of the Pharisees is past; it is time to make the truth of the gospel real in our life. The future of Russia depends on the faith of her people: every politician must learn that truth and make it his own. The best among the *startzi** told me, just before I was turned out of Russia in 1922, that communists and leaders of the Red Army came to confession to him, saying that they put their hope in the action of the Holy Spirit on the heart of the sinful Russian people. There spoke not only a religious voice but a voice far better qualified to call itself national than that of those *émigrés* who look on themselves as true Russian patriots but have no faith in the people of Russia. The words of that monk came to me like a message from another world, a world where there is neither "right-wing" nor "left," warfare neither between political parties

* The plural of *staretz*, literally "old man"; a spiritual director, not necessarily a priest; a special feature of Russian monasticism.—Tr.

for power nor between classes for material aggrandizement. If we would find the needed criterion of our judgements and the needed energy for our actions we must turn our hearts and minds towards this other world. The deceitful idolatry of the State and of nationality must be overcome by the power of religion.

We neither may nor can cut ourselves off from Russia and our people there, from her destiny as a whole. Human destinies have again been made one, they are no longer individually isolated. Individualism is done with. All afflictions and sufferings must be borne to the end in unity with our people and our land. Where are the land and the people, there above all is Russia. The very contact with Russian earth is the beginning of healing, a return to the well-springs of life. That is why the specifically *émigré* psychology is a psychology of sin, the springs of life are dried up for it (this does not mean that such a psychology necessarily exists in all Russians living abroad). Russia can be saved only from within, by the development of vital changes at home. The people do not want to die and are saved by the necessities of life, bolshevist power is forced to adapt itself to life. It is not possible to have faith in the work of Soviet creation, it is an even more horrible nightmare than its work of destruction; it is the system of Shigalev in *The Possessed*, the system of the stud-farm applied to human beings. The power of the bolshevists is impressive only exteriorly: they are really amazingly weak and their works bear the stamp of commonplace vulgarity and weariness; they can only imitate great men. But behind it all there is still the Russian people and nothing can stop them from living on and remaining a great people, endowed with superb gifts: hidden in the depths of Russia the myriad tiny influences are at work, preparing her salvation. And you too can have your part in these vital movements and affect their results if you keep yourselves spiritually in touch with our people and our land.

There is no more amoral saying than "The worse things are, the better it is": such a principle can be accepted only by those who are indifferent both to the worse and to the better. Those who are for Russia and her people can only wish that things may go better, for the end of Bolshevism will come by the amelioration and not by the aggravation of the present state of affairs. Life in Russia is a prolonged torture, a consenting to be sacrificed, to martyrdom, to humiliation; but by this torture, this sacrifice, this martyrdom Russia is satisfying for her sins and working out her salvation: there is already an unbroken spiritual activity, a moral resistance to the poison which taints the very breath of life. But communist authority enforces obedience by means of hunger and other coercion, and it is hard for the weak to resist. I am astonished when I think of the indignant complaints called forth by the notorious tyranny and lack of liberty under the old regime: there was tremendous freedom in those days compared with what we have under the Soviets. Everything will happen differently from what most of the *émigrés* and party-politicians imagine and there will be plenty of surprises. We can hardly suppose that salvation will come from Europe, who has nothing to do with us and is herself nearly at the last gasp. But our freedom will not come whence we expect it but whence God sends it.

The Russians cannot be forced; they must work for their regeneration from within, the revolution must get weaker and weaker till it dies of its own inanition. There is good in the fact that Bolshevism is lasting so long and that it has not been overturned from outside and by force. Instead, the communist idea has discredited itself and lost its halo, so that its venom will not spread and do us mortal injury: our healing is slow, but it is an organic process. It requires in the first place that we should renounce the spirit of falsehood, come out of the realm of phantasms and move towards reality, and at the moment the most urgent need is to strengthen the primacy of spiritual over political activity. The ascendency of politics increases the nightmare and bloodthirstiness against which we must take up spiritual weapons.

The freedom of the human spirit must be saved. Are Christians willing to take Christianity seriously, to order their will towards its realization? Unless they submit themselves to a sublime tension of the spirit, unless they seriously try to follow the way, the truth, and the life, atheistic Communism will triumph everywhere. But the free spirit, the spirit of deliverance, is independent of forces that are successful and in possession. Christianity is going back to the state she enjoyed before Constantine: she has to undertake the conquest of the world afresh.

IV. DEMOCRACY, SOCIALISM AND THEOCRACY

IV. DEMOCRACY, SOCIALISM AND THEOCRACY

I

It is the spiritual first principles of Democracy and Socialism that interest me, and I am consequently not concerned with the study of their modified expressions in the numerous democratic and socialistic forms but with the ultimate boundaries of the types, with their "ideas."

There is a number of transitory stages between Democracy and Socialism, all sorts of *rapprochements* and alliances. One very large party calls itself social-democratic. But the bolshevists very properly got rid of the label "social-democratic" and called themselves communists; that is to say, they went back to the Communist Manifesto. (Marx was a communist and not a social-democrat; he was never a democrat, his tone is essentially anti-democratic.) Scientific Socialism has not been conceived by, and does not present itself to European thought as, a democratic doctrine. Nor was the utopian socialism of Saint-Simon democratic but rather the reverse: it represented a reaction against the French Revolution and often has a kinship with the spirit of Joseph de Maistre. Russian communists are right to emphasize that Democracy and Socialism are in essence opposed to one another. Democratic socialism of the Jaurès sort, based on the declaration of the rights of man and of the citizen, is not true Socialism, but only a semi-socialism which does not embody the socialist idea in its integrity. In the same way our revolutionary socialists and *menshevists** of the right wing are left-wing democrats rather than real socialists.

The character of Democracy is purely formal, it knows nothing of its own essence and, within the limits of its affirmed principle, has no consistency. It does not want to know in what name the people's will is expressed or to subordinate that will to any higher end. If Democracy comes to define the end towards which the people's will should move, if it finds an object worthy of it and is provided with a positive substance, at that moment it is forced to put that end, that object, that substance above the formal principle of the expression of the people's will, and accept them as the basis of society. But this Democracy is not willing to do. It is indifferent to the direction and essence of the popular will, and has no criterion whereby it may judge its tendencies or decide the worth of the will itself. Power in the people's hands is not ordered towards any object, and good and evil are alike indifferent for Demo-

*Two pre-revolutionary Russian political parties whose aims were nearer to Fabianism than to true Socialism.—Tr.

cracy. It is tolerant because of this indifference, because it has lost faith in Truth, because it is totally unable to choose any truth. It is doubting, engendered in an age of doubt: a faithless age whose people have lost the reliable criteria of Truth, who are not strong enough to give their adhesion to any absolute truth whatsoever. It is a complete relativism, the negation of all absolutes.

Democracy is indifferent to truth because it has left its discovery to the votes of a majority, for it is only on the condition of ignoring or not believing in Truth that one can accept quantitative power and revere the opinion of a crowd. Democracy being formalist, sceptical, and without substantial reality it has a completely profane character and is opposed to every society of a sacred type, for Truth is sacred in its very nature and a society founded on it cannot be exclusively secular. This profane Democracy means separation from the ontological foundations of human society, a severance from Truth. It is the essential hypothesis of pure Democracy that society should be organized from a political point of view, as though there were no such thing as Truth, and therein lies the radical lie of its idea: a humanist self-affirmation. The human will must direct human societies, and everything that upsets the expression and absolute domination of this will must be got rid of. That is a denial of spiritual principles that lie more deep than the formal expression of what a people wants, a turning-upside-down of the whole hierarchical structure of society.

An extreme optimism is a condition precedent of Democracy, and democratic scepticism itself is optimist. There is no despair on account of the loss of Truth. It is believed that a mechanical counting of votes must always lead to good results. Behind Democracy stands the optimistic dogma of the natural goodness and loving-kindness proper to human nature. Jean-Jacques Rousseau was the spiritual father of Democracy and it was infected at its roots by his sentimental notions about humanity. It simply will not see that there is also a radical evil in human nature, and does not allow for the fact that the will of the people can follow iniquity, that the majority may be for error and untruth, leaving truth and rightness to a weak minority. There is no guarantee that the general will shall be turned towards the good, that it will seek freedom rather than the complete destruction of freedom. The Revolution in France was begun by the proclamation of the rights and liberty of man; under the Terror all liberty was completely done away with. When, in pure affirmation of itself, the unenlightened popular will refuses to submit itself to any superior being, and claims arbitrarily to direct the destinies of human societies, it easily enters on persecution of Truth, denial of the true, and quenching of all spiritual freedom.

Democracy springs from the *pathos* of liberty, of the affirmation of absolute rights in every man, and it is an affirmation of liberty, of freedom of choice, that is put forward as its rock-bottom truth. Democratic apologists assert that its spiritual origin is the proclamation of liberty of conscience by religious bodies at the time of the Reformation in England. But the concept of a negative liberty, abstract and formalist, hides a poison which has corrupted the historic democracies and developed into the ruin in them of all freedom of spirit. Rousseau denied liberty of conscience in principle; Robespierre destroyed it in fact. An autocratic mob is able to violate human conscience and suppress all power of choice. Tocqueville and John Stuart Mill, who can hardly be called enemies of Democracy, spoke with great disquiet of the dangers of the system as threatening man's freedom and individuality. It is individualist in principle, but its sinister dialectic leads the other way, to a dead-levelling of human beings. Democrats talk a lot about liberty, but no respect for the human spirit and personality is entailed: it is a love of liberty expressed by people who are not interested in Truth.

Democracy is fanatical only at times of revolution. In its normal peaceful state it is innocent of all such excess—but finds a thousand quiet ways of reducing human personalities to uniformity and stifling their free-spiritedness. There was probably more real liberty of spirit in the days when the fires of the Spanish Inquisition were blazing than in the middle-class republics of to-day, wherein spirit and religious conscience are themselves denied. Formalist and sceptical love of liberty has done a very great deal to destroy human "originality" and the variousness of personality, and, so far from involving freedom of spirit and of choice, these freedoms simply cannot exist in a democratic society.

Democracy was born just when the organic unity of a common will was breaking up, when society was disintegrating and when the popular beliefs by which people were united were dying. The doctrine of the supremacy and autocracy of the general will appeared at the moment when there had ceased to be a general will. Democracy is a system peculiar to a critical and not to an organic period in social life. It in fact sets out to put together again the will of a disunited people; but for it human personality is only an abstraction, no more important than any other, and the task of unifying men is simply a mechanical one. The number of votes of those who agree is counted—but the verdict is not the organic will of a people, for that is a thing that cannot be gauged by arithmetic or proved by the volume of voices. That will is shown in the whole history of a nation and by the character of its general culture. But it finds its expression before all and above all in its religious life: a single and common will cannot be found outside that organic domain, the unity of religious belief.

When a true general will fails the people are resolved into individual units and it is impossible again to make a unity of them: there remains only the arithmetical sum of the wishes of the majority and of the minority. Party strife begins, contentions between classes and groups, and a sort of unity can be got only by the way of compromise. Democracy is the arena of these struggles and chaotic conflicts of interests. There is no agreement, no stability; everything is weak and uncertain: it is an endless state of transition. Democracy institutes parliaments, which are the least organic of all constitutions, instruments of the dictatorship of political gangs. This ephemeral society needs something which is not to be found in Democracy; real metaphysical life is beyond its limits, it stops short at a formal and unsubstantial freedom to choose. So it is that monarchists and socialists, in their different ways, weaken the life of democratic societies, for both demand that the choice should be specified, its object made clear.

Democracy recognizes the autocratic sovereignty of the people, but it ignores the people itself. There *is* no "people" in a democracy: for that name cannot be given to a single generation, disassociated from its past, belonging only to the passing moment, and not even the whole of the contemporary generation but just those parts that look on themselves as arbiters of destiny. The people is a great historical whole which includes all its generations, not only of the living but also of the dead, of our fathers and our forebears. The will of the Russian people is the will of a thousand years of people, of those who were baptized under St. Vladimir, who built up Russia under the great Muscovite princes, who found their way out of the troubles of the seventeenth century, who opened a window on to Europe under Peter the Great, who have given great saints and heroes for the veneration of the world, who formed a huge empire and a fine literary culture. The passing wish of one generation which has broken with its past is not the will of a people. The presumptuous self-confidence and contempt of its ancestors' values manifested by the present age is precisely the rooted falsehood in Democracy which entails a break between past, present, and future, the denial of eternity, and the worship of a destructive modernism. When the future of Russia is under consideration we must listen to the voice of all her people at all times: legend, history, and tradition, the voice of generations now passed into eternity, all contribute to the formation of a common organic will. Of this Democracy takes no heed, and in consequence knows nothing of a people's will: it knows only the wishes of an insignificant handful of contemporary individuals.

The crisis for Democracy began long ago. The first disappointment was provided by the failure of the French Revolution to fulfil its promises. To-day democracies are in a wretched state of weakness and discontent, torn by interior dissensions, without life or promise for the future. They stand for liberty only in the sense of indifference to good and evil, truth and falsehood, and now have begun to doubt the use and rightness of mechanical universal suffrage. Some look for help in corporate representation, in a return to the mediaeval institution of gilds, hoping thereby to attain an organic unity in which men will no longer be separated units only. This crisis of democracy is completely in accordance with its formalist and unmetaphysical character. The thing to be seriously studied is the essence of a people's will, what makes it right, true, and holy. That the wish of each one should be formally expressed, and that a quantitative majority determines the policy of a society in conformity with a given direction of those wishes, does not matter. What does matter is the ultimate end of the will of the people and the quality of that will. Socialism subjects Democracy to keenly adverse criticism, uncovers its fundamental weakness, and opposes to it a real will qualitatively defined. Socialists seek social justice and it is to be attained in an objectively determined way; and their principles are diametrically opposed to Democracy.

II

Socialism is essentially material, and it knows what it wants. It does not think that what the popular will is after is a matter of indifference, and does not accept or abandon anything at its whim. It seeks the true and does not leave the answer to the question "What is Truth?" to a counting of votes. Psychologically, Socialism is not sceptical; on the contrary, it is a faith and claims to be a new power at the service of humanity. Utopian Saint-Simonism and scientific Marxism are equally imbued with religious pretensions, putting forward a complete philosophy of life for the resolution of all its problems. The will in Socialism is much more unbending, more unwaveringly directed, and with a greater integrity than in Democracy: it has one only and all-embracing object. By its nature Socialism has no use for parliaments, institutions for the free discussion of opinions and the clash of party interests. It recognizes the popular will in the object of that will. It does not uphold the formal sovereignty of a people or a nation but the material sovereignty of an elect class: an elect class whose right, true, and holy will has special virtues.

Socialism is messianic. There is only one elect class, the people of the covenant, the proletariat. It alone is free from the original sin which vitiates all history and all the so-called bourgeois culture, the sin of the exploitation of man by man and class by class. This messiah-class is the very embryo of true humanity, the humanity of the future to which exploitation will be unknown. The proletariat is the new Israel, and all the attributes of God's chosen people are transferred to it; it is to be the liberator and redeemer of mankind, and to establish the Kingdom of God on earth. So in this latter day the old Hebrew millenarism has come to life again in a secular shape. The chosen class will at last realize on earth the promised kingdom, the happiness in Israel, that the crucified Messiah has not done. The proletariat is the new messiah, organizer of an earthly kingdom, in whose name the former Messiah was rejected because he preached a kingdom that is not of this world.

The sovereignty of the proletariat sets itself up against the sovereignty of the people: the proletariat is the only true people, the righteous ones who have all the qualities needful for the right ordering of the will towards a higher kind of life. Real life, the fulness of life, is in our days a privilege of the proletariat alone. It is a class which is victorious as well as oppressed, and it is its destiny to bring to pass the supreme domination of humanity: it will reduce the forces of nature under control once and for all and develop productive powers to their maximum. The assuming of power by this class will mark the change-over from the rule of necessity to the rule of liberty, a world-wide convulsion; then and only then will the history of humanity really begin: "super-history." Such are the hopes of classical revolutionary Socialism, and they are more interesting and instructive than the transitory and unfinished forms of Social-democracy with its opportunist adaptation to bourgeois life.

Nevertheless, it would be wrong to suppose that, according to Socialist thought, sovereignty should appertain to the actual effective proletariat as to a body of human beings. Sovereignty does not belong to the proletariat as to a "fact" but to the proletariat as to an "idea"; the "idea of the proletariat" must have world dominion. In this sense, then, Socialism is not an empirical realism but an idealism. The mission of guarding the proletarian idea is confided to a minority elected by the spirit of history, forming a group of those sentient ones who know and understand the true faith; and this chosen group holds the plenitude of power. Thus Socialism is in its way aristocratic, and certainly not democratic. In the name of the "idea," in the name of the true proletarian will whose expression can be entrusted only to a small number, in the name of proletarian interests, which are equally the interests of the whole human race but which few men recognize and know, in the name of these every sort of violence may be inflicted on the actual living proletarian people. This unenlightened human mob may be compelled to a realization of the "proletarian idea" by machine-guns, bayonets, and whips. But the anti-democracy of Socialism goes further than rejection of the sovereignty of the people and of the right of every citizen to share in the free expression of its will. It does not allow such expression even to the elect, the proletarian class which directs the will of the people. This right belongs only to an *élite*, namely, to those workers who are socialist-minded: and not just socialist but *really* socialist, that is, for example, "bolshevist-minded" and not just "I.L.P.-minded." All those workers who are not open to the proletarian idea, who have not an essentially socialist mentality, may and ought to be deprived of any right to express their views and to take part in the management of social life. Thus is justified in principle the dictatorship exercised by a minority of official guardians of the pure socialist idea over a majority which remains in outer darkness. It follows from the *pathos*, the pseudo-messianism, of this revolutionary Socialism that it cannot but be an advocate of dictatorship. In notable contrast with Democracy it gives fulness of power and hands over autocratic authority only to a will of a determined kind, one that is socialist, that is, true and just. It is by its very essence intolerant and exclusive: by virtue of its very "idea" it cannot allow any freedom to its opponents and those who think differently; there is a strict obligation on it to refuse liberty of conscience. It is the system of Dostoievsky's Grand Inquisitor and of his Shigalev. Its way is to settle the destiny of human society by denying freedom to the human spirit.

The socialist state and society are of the type of a religious denomination, not secular and civil but sacred. It does not profess indifference to religions, as a liberal-democratic state does, but defines the truth of a certain faith and imposes it by force, so that there is a dominant creed, and those who accept it must be privileged. Those who do not accept it must find themselves in a situation analogous to that of the Jews in the old Christian theocratic societies. The socialist state claims to be a sacred state, infused by the grace, not indeed of God, but of Satan—but still a grace.

Socialism denies liberty to conscience just as, in effect, the Catholic theocracy of the middle ages denied it. It seeks to coerce men to truth and virtue, so that the individual is deprived of that liberty of choice, that free election, that liberal Democracy requires. The fallacious pretension of mediaeval theocratic imperialism, the idea of an external and artificial union of mankind, a quantitative universality, reappears in Socialism. Socialist utopias, which are the golden dreams of so many people, have never held out any promise of liberty: rather have they always been put forward as absolutely despotic organizations wherein liberty should be utterly destroyed. The free circulation of people from one place to another was scarcely easier in the utopia of Sir Thomas More than during the harder years of the Soviet Socialist Republic. In Cabet's utopia only one newspaper appeared, the government journal: any publications of a free press were utterly forbidden. We used to pay too little attention to utopias, or even disregarded them altogether, saying with regret that they were impossible of realization. Now, indeed, they seem to be able to be brought about far more easily than we supposed, and we are actually faced by an agonizing problem of quite another kind: how can we prevent their final realization? We Russians used to look on the bolshevists as utopians, out of touch with real life; the constitutional-democrats were the realists. Experience has taught us that the constitutional-democrats were the fantastic theorists. They dreamed of a legal constitution for Russia; of rights and liberties for men and citizens—in the conditions of Russian life: senseless dreaming, impossible paradise! The bolshevists have shown themselves the true realists: they saw which was the easiest way and followed the line of least resistance, they were *minimalists* rather than *maximalists*. They adapted their policy as well as they could to the interests and impulses of the masses and to the Russian traditions concerning the exercise of power. Utopias are more realizable than those "realist politics" that are only the carefully calculated policies of office-holders, and towards utopias we are moving. But it is possible that a new age is already beginning, in which cultured and intelligent people will dream of ways to avoid ideal states and to get back to a society that is less "perfect" and more free. We shall give up our socialist dreams—for it is not only the socialist that has them. Russian liberals also used to believe that there was nothing better than Socialism but that unhappily it was impracticable, that our degree of heroism was insufficient to realize so high an ideal. Now we dream of an imperfect and freer regime.

It appears that liberty is bound up with imperfection, with a right to imperfection. Socialism leads to the same type of authoritarian state as Theocracy involves. The amazing intuition of Leontiev, who foresaw and predicted the triumph of a bolshevist revolution in Russia, maintained that the age-long tradition of submission and the old instinct of obedience would have to be utilized by Socialism: he knew that human blood and not rose-water would be the liquid of its cement. Herein he showed himself a great deal wiser than that majority of Russians who for a hundred years dreamed the socialist idyll and imagined that it meant freedom. No; one must choose: either Socialism or liberty of spirit, the liberty of man's conscience. The genius of Dostoievsky saw this clearly enough. Socialism uses a "sacred" authority and establishes a "sacred" society in which there is no place for the "lay," for the free, for choice, for the unrestricted activity of human forces.

Socialism wants in its power the whole of man, soul as well as body, and aims at control over the most intimate places of the spirit. Here is an imitation of the claims of the Christian Church. Hitherto the Church alone has claimed a dominion over the human soul and undertaken to direct it; the State knew its own limits and had no such ambition: it could imprison people and put them to death but it did not look for internal spiritual submission. This is true of the secular state; but the theocratic state, with its universal claims and pretension to the sacred privileges of a church, did look for such submission. So does the Socialism of the communists. It aims at drilling souls in platoons, disciplining them till they are quite content in their human ant-hill, till they like a barrack-life and no longer look for spiritual liberty; it wants to produce a race of contented children, unaware of sin. Christianity clings first and foremost to the freedom of the human spirit, and will not allow the possibility of drilling mankind into the earthly paradise. It leaves the attempt to Antichrist.

Socialism is right in putting the substantial object of the people's will above the will itself and above its formal expression. If there be any substantive value and last end in the life of a people, then that value and end ought to be put before everything else. Thus absolute values are affirmed and a valid object offered for attainment. But a spiritual life alone can be the proper end of human life, only the divine reality can give reality to it. Consequently, the spiritual objects of religion must be made the primary principle of human societies and given a place before all self-affirmation of the human will. The integral freedom of man can be safeguarded only by recognition of these religious ends and by submission to the divine will; human licence and despotism are simply destructive of human liberty. It is appalling for men to be entirely subject to the authority of men, to be domineered over by human masses which do not submit themselves to any higher truth. So we come up against the inevitable need to put boundaries to democratic autocracy, just as to any human autocracy, monarchist or other. Socialism represents the ultimate goal of Humanism, the crisis of the human self-affirmation formulated by Democracy. It has already gone on to another inhuman thing, to that collectivism in whose name everything human must be offered up as a sacrifice. Marx was against humanity: in him self-affirmation was turned into the negation of man. Democracy is still on the side of man; Socialism has already got beyond all that. It is a reaction against the history of the modern world and a return to the middle ages—but in the name of another god. The new middle ages must resemble the old and have its inverted theocracy. But when the reign of secular Humanism finally comes to an end we shall see the gulf of contradiction. The socialist state has a semblance to theocracy—because it is a government by Satan. In it collectivist society has become a ruler more absolute and more terrible than the tyrants of Assyria and Persia.

III

Vladimir Soloviev used to say that to overcome Socialism it is necessary first to see the truth that is in it. Socialism cannot be fought with "bourgeois ideas"; it is useless to set over against it the middle-class, democratic, capitalist society of the nineteenth and twentieth centuries. It is precisely this bourgeois society that has bred Socialism and involved us in it. Socialism is flesh of the flesh and blood of the blood of Capitalism. They both belong to the same world; they are animated by a common spirit—or rather, by a common negation of spirit. Socialism has inherited the middle-class atheism of the capitalist nineteenth-century, which was, indeed, the most atheistical society known to history. It falsified the relation between man and man, and between man and physical nature. Its political economy corrupted the hierarchical organization of society and gave birth to economic materialism, which is an exact reflection of the actual state of that nineteenth-century civilization. The life of the spirit became almost less than an accident, a speculative adaptation to less high things. The worship of Mammon instead of God is a characteristic of Socialism as well as of Capitalism. Socialism is no longer an utopia or a dream: it is an objective threat, and a warning to Christians to show them unmistakably that they have not fulfilled the word of Christ, that they have in effect apostatized. A basis is sometimes assigned to Capitalism by the statement that human nature is sinful and that sin cannot be got rid of by force, while the essence of Socialism is in the supposition that this nature is entirely good. But it is forgotten that the moment of history can come when the evil in human nature, namely, the sin in which it is involved, will have taken on a new shape. It is the sinful part of our nature that begets Socialism. Capitalism, considered spiritually and morally, arose because human nature is prone to evil. But Socialism has arisen for exactly the same reason. Apostasy from the Christian faith, abandonment of spiritual principles and disregard of the spiritual ends of life, must of necessity lead first to the stage called Capitalism and then to the stage called Socialism. It follows clearly enough that we must begin to make our Christianity effectively real by a return to the life of the spirit, that a normal hierarchical harmony of life must be recovered, that that which is economic must be subordinated to that which is spiritual, that politics must be again confined within their proper limits.

Socialism claims to have substantial being and a last end, even a true being and a right end. (There it differs from Democracy, which is patient of all substances and all ends.) The socialistic substance of life and the socialistic end of life are such that they excite their disciples to fanaticism. But what are they? Purely fictitious. Socialism is as lacking in substance, as little ontological, as Democracy. What is there in Socialism that must be regarded as the reality and end of life (and not simply as means and motives) that is not at the same time found outside of Socialism? Socialization of the means of production is certainly not the reality and end of life. There is nothing to be found in economics which has to do with the ends of, and not the means to, life. Economic equality is not such an end, any more than is the organized productive labour that Socialism has divinized. This divinization of labour at the expense of qualitative values has led to complete disregard of the end and meaning of life. Socialism has obtained so much importance in these days because the ends of human life became obscured, and were then definitely replaced by the means to life. This confusion was brought about in the bourgeois civilization of the last century, in its economics: the exterior organization of life swallowed up everything else. The substantial values and end of life can be looked for only in a spiritual reality, in a *cultus* of the soul, for they are simply and solely of a spiritual order; they do not belong to a social order, they cannot be imagined under political and economic forms. No system of social and political ideas can have a true substance unless it finds it in the life of the spirit, in the subordination of all social and political forms to a spiritual end.

The substance of Socialism is only apparent. Its deadly dialectic can only demonstrate the absence of all spiritual reality from contemporary civilization. The "idea of the proletariat," in whose name so much blood has been poured out and which excites so fanatical a devotion, is seen to be an idea that has no background. It talks about the means to life, but tells us nothing about life itself—for Socialism is incapable of reaching out to life's ends. The pitiable chatter about the new proletarian soul and the new proletarian culture produces a certain feeling of uneasiness even among socialists themselves. There is no sign of the birth of a new soul: she remains the old soul of the old Adam, full of greed, envy, anger, and the spirit of revenge. The only new thing about this soul is the fact that her sense of sin is weakened and repentance has become more difficult for her. There is no sign of a new proletarian culture, there is no new proletarian achievement. Socialism thrives on middle-class culture and draws its intellectual nourishment from the materialism of bourgeois prophets.

There is, however, something new in Socialism—the phenomenon of an inhuman collectivism, a new Leviathan. And all the ends and real values of life are swallowed up in this malignant and terrifying collectivism, all spiritual culture is wiped out: such a monster has not got a new human soul, for it has got no human soul at all. The doctrine of Democracy and Socialism informs us that a real and right will may be recognized in the people by means of simple exterior indications, social and political. *There is no such thing as a right will apart from righteousness of the will, apart from sanctity of the will even.* For the human will, the general will, to realize a just life, and for that life to be formed by Truth, it is necessary actually to attain righteousness, to defeat sin, to accept an inpouring of light, and to undergo a change. No exterior sign, no deceptive substitute, may take the place of this; no disguise, no changing of clothes, is the slightest help, for the same substance, or rather the same lack of substance, is covered by the trappings of bourgeois and socialist alike. It is in the first place a religious problem that confronts all societies and all peoples. For the enlightening and transforming of the will, the ordering of it towards divine objects, is a task of religion and not of social polity; and all social and political problems must be subordinated to this religious one.

The substance of life can only be religious. It is an entering into the life of God, that is, into true Being. The will of the people, the proletarian will, is a sinful will; it therefore pertains to not-being and can bring about only a kingdom of not-being. That will must bow before the supreme will, the holy will of God. Thus alone can it attain to being. Sovereignty does not belong to the people or to the proletariat but to God, to Truth himself; and in the life of a society or of a state it is not our will but God's that must be sought. This truth must be upheld against those of "the right," conservatives and traditionalists, as much as against those of "the left," radicals and socialists; for we may not confront democratism with an expression of the human will wrung out of it by privileged groups of mankind.

But enlightenment and change of heart, the fulfilment of the divine will and the divine truth, do not form simply a personal problem for each individual soul to solve: it is equally a social and historical task, confronting whole peoples. Spiritual forces, divine energies, work upon countries and races, on all history, as well as on each one of us personally; it is a matter of change and spiritual revelation in the life of nations: the individual and society cannot be separated and isolated the one from the other. And so we come to the question of Theocracy. Can the problem which has been posed find its solution in a society of the theocratic type?

IV

First Democracy, then Socialism, arose in Europe because the old theocracies had decayed from within. It was inevitable. And mankind makes the journey from one extreme to the other on the same road. The failure to realize Theocracy successfully of necessity led to the democratic and socialistic experiments. One after another the historic defeats took place, and the reason of failure was always the same whatever the type of society concerned: external and formal signs took the place of the needed real change of heart, the spiritual transfiguration. Theocracy was avowedly symbolist whereas Socialism is avowedly materialist, but in either case it is only the outward signs of the sought-for perfection that are attained, not the real thing itself. The old theocracies, the social reign of the Papacy in the West, of the Holy Empire in the East, failed and decayed because they manifested the Kingdom of God on earth only by visible symbols; they never actualized it; the church-state lost more and more of its quality of sacredness and gradually degenerated into a counterfeit Kingdom. The theocratic plan of the middle ages is one of the most superbly grand ideas in history. But it did not take into consideration the fact that there must be a free consent of the human spirit if the Kingdom of Christ is to be realized on earth; that Kingdom cannot be imposed by force. The search for liberty sent mankind along the road towards Democracy. Man began to measure himself by himself, autonomously; thence he went on to affirm himself by virtue of himself; and that affirmation has ended in self-destruction, the extermination of man by himself. That is the tragedy of modern history. The passage from rule-by-another to rule-of-oneself was bound to take place; a society based on external control cannot last for ever, for the autonomous conscience must assert itself sooner or later. But rule-of-oneself ought to lead to rule-by-God, to a higher state of the soul in which she freely accepts and subjects herself to the divine will.

In fact, autonomy has not developed into rule-by-God but collapsed into a rule-by-none, wherein autonomy feeds on itself and becomes the worst of heteronomies. That is what we see in Socialism. In the former theocratic societies rule-by-God was sought but not attained. In contemporary autonomous societies there is no question of rule-by-God, and that is why they have no ontological significance. Past ages were full of sacred symbolism and, in spite of everything, its spiritual value was retained up to a certain time, with an enormous influence in the education and government of Christian peoples. But the time had to come when people wanted to go on to greater realities. Then, however, they did not pass from symbolism to a mystical and ontological realism, the realism of enlightenment and transfiguration, but to an illusory realism, experimental and even materialistic. This sort of realism has no spiritual significance, it is concerned entirely with outward manifestations and not at all with the realization of Being. The one only way to true theocracy, the Kingdom of God, is to work for its effective realization, that is, for the achievement of a deeper spiritual life, for the enlightening and transfiguration of man and of the world.

There is no possibility of a perfect society and a perfect culture without this real spiritual life, that is, without a religious rebirth. We cannot be content with symbolizing or simulating it; we must have the actual thing. But the characteristic indications of the attainment of such a spiritual life are not over-obvious. That is why it is said that the Kingdom of God "cometh not with observation." A too obvious achievement of the Kingdom should excite suspicion, for it may well indicate an imposture. There can be no going-back to the old theocracies of East and West, for there can be no exterior manifestation of God's Kingdom without its precedent effective realization. The sham "Christian state" is of no further use, for it is precisely this state which collapsed and gave us Democracy and Socialism. How then can a real Christian society be established?

Only by religious enlightenment and complete change of heart and will. Perhaps great trials and catastrophes are leading us in that direction. But the true Christian state will be a State no more. What is needed is not to spread ourselves abroad, to display the signs and symbols of an interior life, but to steep ourselves in true spirituality, to come back to the fatherland of the spirit. That would be a more profound revolution than any that the activities of external revolutionaries can bring about.

All systems of ideas and political and social forms throughout the world are going through a period of crisis. They are all in practice worn out and there is no longer anything that rouses the enthusiasm of civilized peoples. The Russians alone still display a colossal energy—for destruction—in their attempt to bring about the maddest of all utopias. Spasmodic efforts are made to buttress the tottering old societies, wherein there are still shreds of theocratic sanctions; but it is an hopeless undertaking. *There is no possibility of a restoration of the theocratic state of the old type, because it never effectively realized the Truth of God; it only looked as if it did from the outside.* Soloviev attributed the fall of Byzantium to her not having even attempted to translate Christianity into life. The same can be said, with variations of particulars, of the other similar states: the germ of their mortal sickness was always within them. Christianity has not failed; but the work of Constantine the Great *has* failed, for all its providential importance and significance. Christianity is coming back to its pre-Constantinian situation, so to say; that is the position in which the Russian Orthodox Church actually is already. It may well be that Christians are being called to go further back yet, to the catacombs, and from there to conquer the world anew. There is little chance that the new empire of the Caesars will want to be Christian, and no fresh initiation of the Christian-state will achieve anything genuine. We are entering an epoch of ill-omened revelations and we must fearlessly face-up to realities. And there is found the meaning of our unhappy joyless age. Christian recognition of evil has been insistent throughout history, and we also must refuse all consoling illusions and sugary optimism. On the other hand, this relative pessimism need not weaken our striving towards the heights of spirituality: the shattering of external illusions is a definite aid to an interior life.

The atheistical and hypocritical civilization of the nineteenth and twentieth centuries celebrates its triumphs at the same time that its principles are most seriously threatened. It begot the World War, an offspring of its own limitless desires, and that war was the beginning of its end. People dream uselessly of a peaceful bourgeois life, of a return to that solid middle-class civilization which they look upon as an almost perfect condition of society. But those unexpected catastrophes, wars and revolutions, were contained in the essence of pre-war civilization and only the most foolish would want to go back to it, though at a first glance their folly may seem logical. The tragedy of the contemporary mess is that nobody in his heart and soul now believes in any political system or social theory. Only Communism still tries to hold its ground, at the cost of a terrific strain on the will and a bloody fanaticism; but it weakens under the deadly blows which it inflicts on its own "idea." Monarchies fall and democracies seem to be at the point of death, the old conceptions of the state and national economy break down; Europe begins to find herself in a condition very similar to that at the beginning of the middle ages. Democracy has ceased to be a political matter and has become a religious and cultural problem: the spiritual rebirth of society and the re-education of the people. The democracies enunciated the freedom of choice, but have not been able to keep their balance on that principle; they must turn to, must choose, must submit themselves to, some absolute truth. And that takes us a long way from Democracy. Its sole justification would be that it is called on to conquer itself: that would be its truth. But everything goes to show that contemporary democracies are decayed and corrupt and that nobody believes in them any longer. Democrats blow neither hot nor cold, and God will spew them out of his mouth.

True life cannot be attained by means of numbers alone. The monarchical principle has had much worth in the past, but monarchists are moved by negative and feeble opinions and often by hate and desire for revenge; for a very large number of them Monarchy is only a useful weapon for the recovery of the privileges of which they have been deprived. It has become impracticable to submit people to a king by the methods used hitherto. They must first of all want him voluntarily; but in that case it would be a quite new kind of monarchy.

Economically and socially Capitalism is infected to death by its own poison. There can be no thought of a revival of the industrial-capitalist regime that has brought the war and so many other disasters upon mankind; but the hope of substituting the socialist for the capitalist system has been taken away as well. We have lost belief in that too. For Socialism is no longer invisible, an object of faith; we can see it and, in so far as it is an applied and knowable system, it is in as bad a way as Capitalism itself: it drags human society up a completely blind alley. The economic life of a people is determined by the moral philosophy of work, the reasons on account of which men work, but these moral foundations are overturned and we are threatened with famine. Something irrevocable has happened which will make impossible the constraint of men to the discipline of work that obtained under Capitalism, and nothing is less fitted than Socialism to provide a new discipline and moral basis. It divinizes work, makes an idol of it, and disintegrates it completely, at the same time destroying that working-class in whose name all sorts of bloody violences are perpetrated. The contemporary economic question, just as much as the political question, has become a spiritual one, and it cannot be resolved by mankind alone. The restoration of work to its right place in man's life presupposes a spiritual rebirth; but Socialism is as powerless as Capitalism to save us, not only because of its economic incapacity but also because of its spiritual depravity: its essential satanism is apparent. The failure of Socialism is as intense as that of all other social systems, and it will be the final great crash before we enter on the new way.

There is such a thing as a Christian socialism (too much importance must not be given to names; I am quite ready to label myself a Christian socialist), but to call it that is rather a misuse of words. Christian socialism is not true Socialism, and real socialists will have nothing to do with it. Socialism in the proper sense of the word is the movement which tries to make human society mistress of her destiny by external means and physical forces. That is certainly not Christian socialism. The latter merely recognizes the injustices of the individualistic capitalist system. The trouble is that the old Christian socialism is a rather anaesthetic business, with nothing radical in its composition, and so can have very little influence. Christianity has got to take a much deeper and wider view of this matter of life in society.

Faith in the ultimate political and social salvation of mankind is quenched. We have reached settlement-day after a series of centuries during which movement was from the centre, the spiritual core of life, to the periphery, its surface and social exterior. And the more empty of real significance social life has become, the more it has tyrannized over the general life of man. Politics have twined about us like a strangling parasite, and the greater part of contemporary political and social life has no reality, no being, at all: it is just bogus. The strife of parties, parliaments, conferences, newspapers, programmes and platforms, propaganda and demonstrations, the grab and scheming for power—these are not life, they have no point of contact with its essence and end, they are a hopeless hindrance. The world needs a strong reaction from this domination by exterior things, a change back in favour of interior spiritual life, not only for the sake of individuals but for the sake of real metaphysical life itself. To many who are caught up in the web of modern activities this must sound like an invitation to suicide. But we have got to choose. The life of the spirit is either a sublime reality or an illusion: accordingly we have either to look for salvation in it rather than in the fuss of politics, or else dismiss it altogether as false. When it seems that everything is over and finished, when the earth crumbles away under our feet as it does to-day, when there is neither hope nor illusion, when we can see all things naked and undeceiving, then is the acceptable time for a religious quickening in the world. We are at that time: Dostoievsky recognized it, Soloviev recognized it, and we should do well to recognize it too, fully and unflinchingly. It is in the tradition of Russian thought to understand these things, and the revolution of 1917 can help us to. It took place when liberal Democracy in Russia had proved itself powerless and that modern emphasis on man had reached its limit; consequently, its place was taken by an absolute and anti-humanist Socialism. The Russian people, in full accordance with their particular mentality, offered themselves as a burnt-offering on the altar of an experiment unknown to previous history: they have demonstrated the extremest consequences of certain ideas. They are an apocalyptic people and they could not stop short at a compromise, some "humanitarian state": they had to make real either brotherhood in Christ or comradeship in Antichrist. If the one does not reign, then the other will. The people of Russia have put this choice before the whole world with awe-inspiring force.

THE "GENERAL LINE" OF SOVIET PHILOSOPHY

THE "GENERAL LINE" OF SOVIET PHILOSOPHY

I

I HAVE lately had occasion to read a number of Soviet works relating to the philosophy and anti-religious propaganda of 1931, the very latest word of the communists on the subject.* It is not attractive reading, but it is interesting and instructive.

There is in process of formation in Soviet Russia a synthetic philosophical system which represents Marx-Leninism as enriched by experience gained during the constructive period of the revolution, revolutionary experience being the source of philo-

* Principally, *Militant Atheism* (1931), the communist philosophical and scientific review, which includes an important chronicle of Western intellectual currents; *Historical Materialism* (1931), published by the board of authors of the Institute of Professors of Red Philosophy under the direction of Raltsev, a work of capital importance as an encyclopædia of Marx-Leninism; *Towards Conversion on the Philosophic Front* (1931); *Antireligious*, a review of scientific method (1931); *Collection of Programmes and Methods in Preparation for Renewed Antireligious Activity*; *On Religion*, by Lenin; *The Antireligious Front*, by Yaroslavsky (1924); *The War against Class and Religion*, by Khudiakov. I was unfortunately not able to consult the review called *Under the Flag of Marxism*, which represents, not the "general line," but Deborin's group. I do not name, assuming them to be known, the classical Marxist works, such as those of Plekhanov, Bogdanov, Bukharin, and others who are at present rejected. For long the leading treatise was Bukharin's *Theory of Historical Materialism*. It is now regarded as heretical and dangerous, representing the right-wing or *kulak* deviation in the Communist Party.

sophical knowledge. Such research is given a definite place in the work of building up the socialist-soviet state. Capital importance is accorded to the elaboration of an integral philosophy; for several years there has been a college given over to the study of Hegel's Logic, a thing that would be difficult to establish among the *émigrés*. The "general line" of philosophy emerged from discussions which went on over a period of five years. The least political divergences within the Communist Party (to the "right," of Bukharin, to the "left," of Trotsky) are attributed to philosophical error. The young Soviet philosophers protest energetically against any tendency to bring philosophy and the natural sciences together as a heterodox deviation. The enslavement of thought is unprecedented and stupefying, but it is a bondage that is freely accepted and liked. These young people are sincerely taken with the idea: they are believers, men who know not doubt. Such dogmatism, such a total absence of scepticism, are well calculated to surprise the Westerner; Christians themselves have not so unquestioning a faith, probably because of the importance of spiritual freedom to Christianity. The young Soviet students of philosophy are better equipped than one would expect, they have precise, but one-sided, knowledge and their general level is pretty high; they are well armed to defend their faith and to attack their opponent's. They have a "doctrine of the schools" and in that respect resemble

Catholics. But there are no great names, no outstanding figures, no personalities; their thought is purely anonymous. The word of Dostoievsky comes to mind, "We shall smother all geniuses in their cradles."

Philosophical work is done by the nameless "collective" which elaborates the "general line" under higher direction: a real five-year plan in the sector of philosophy. In order that this plan may be fulfilled, theory has to be closely associated with practice, with the work of the economic building-up of Socialism. Soviet philosophy is not truly philosophy at all. Philosophy is essentially problematical and supposes liberty of thought; its discovery of truth is the term of a series of constructive operations of knowledge. Soviet philosophy is a theology: it has its revelation, its holy books, its ecclesiastical authority, its official teachers; it supposes the existence of one orthodoxy and innumerable heresies. Marx-Leninism has been transformed into a scholasticism *sui generis*, and the defence of orthodoxy, that is, of eternal truth in its integrity, and the distinguishing of heresies has attained a degree of refinement difficult for the uninitiated to imagine. The one end of all this speculation is the establishment of the "general line" of Marx-Leninism. In Soviet Russia philosophical discussion is not an untrammeled search for truth, it does not at all recall the Platonic dialogues, it is not a battleground of different opinions from which truth may emerge: it consists in convicting of heresy and excommunicating heretics.

Everyone engaged in this work lives in fear, not knowing what will be the heresies of to-morrow. Most of the old Marxists have been excommunicated: Plekhanov, Bogdanov, Lunatcharsky, Deborin, Bukharin, Trotsky, Riazanov; Kautsky and Kunov among the Westerners. The orthodox line comprises Marx, Engels, Lenin, and Stalin. You are lost if you put in this line of Marxist tradition any of those who, like Plekhanov or Kautsky, formerly had authority but have since been revealed as traitors. It is an absolute obligation to look on Lenin as a great philosopher who did much to advance Marxism. The directions of the Communist Party are the basis of philosophical work, and this work is carried on in an atmosphere of continual nervousness of falling into heresy; the workers hold themselves in readiness to abandon their views at any moment if they are not in accordance with the "general line." Any right to individual critical reflection is refused, only collective criticism is possible. Obviously we are here dealing with a strictly conservative mentality, a mentality in which there is implicit consent to authority and to direction from above, wherein creative initiative and liberty of thought are rejected, and which affirms the immutability of the foundations on which its thought is based.

There is less concern to establish the dogmas of

Marxist truth than to excommunicate those who stray from it. It does not occur naturally to the mind of anybody that Marxism and Leninism can themselves be objects of examination and investigation, that they can be called in question: this attitude is called "restatement" and is severely punished. One of the participants in these philosophical beginnings wrote a book on the origins of religion, and he found himself taken to task because he said nothing of Lenin's views on totemism and magic. He answered in despair that he did not know what to say, because there is not a line about those subjects in Lenin's works! It was complained against another author that he had mentioned the names of bourgeois men of learning in his text, but those of Marx and Engels only in the footnotes! When accused of the "mechanicist" heresy, he pleaded in vain that he could not change his convictions in a day, asked for time to reconsider them, declared that as a loyal man he had already recanted everything. . .

The arguments in these debates can always be reduced to citations from the holy scriptures; Lenin *dixit*, it is written in Marx. . . . And yet Lenin himself wrote: "We do not want anything to be accepted with the eyes shut, to be an article of faith. Everyone should keep his head tight on his own shoulders, and think out and verify everything for himself." Lenin himself thought as an individual and not as a part of the "collectivity" which he created, but these words of his have not taken root. On the other hand, a large part of Russia has adopted his coarseness of language, as when he said that "Dialectical materialism throws the idealist swine who defend God on to the dung-heap." He professed a deep respect for Hegel and read his Logic assiduously, making marginal notes which have been published as a manual of philosophy. When Hegel defends the idea of God, Lenin writes, "You felt pity for this poor little godlet, you idealist swine." That is the style of nearly all the anti-religious propagandist writing. In practice, collectivist thought, which alone can exercise authority, makes use of informers, spies, and secret reports: philosophy is a monopoly of the government, intellectual speculation is an administrative department. Lenin supplies the norms not only of philosophy, but even of physics; the inspired chief of the proletariat must be an inspired theorist as well. The whole of philosophical speculation from end to end consists only of appreciation and estimation in terms of orthodoxy and heresy, so that there can be no free flow of thought. Any "restatement" of Marxism constitutes a "modernist" attitude that is even more hateful to Marx-Leninists than theological Modernism is to Catholics. What is even more remarkable is that Stalin, who is far from a genius and knows nothing of philosophy, is no less a source of philosophical direction. Thus the system of controlled work when applied to philosophy leads to a denial of all individuality of thought; young thinkers are continually required to abandon all personal views and to repudiate any work which shows the slightest deviation from the received teaching. At a meeting of the Communist Academy, Deborin underwent a harassing cross-examination from Yaroslavsky that exactly resembled an interrogatory by the G.P.U. Deborin is a disciple of Plekhanov, a former menshevist, and he once wrote some articles that could be interpreted unfavourably to Lenin and Bolshevism. The unfortunate man acknowledged his guilt, but that was not enough; he had again to stigmatize his past opinions, to conduct a severe self-criticism, to metaphorically flog himself in public. He at first tried to justify himself, alleging that what he had written in 1906-7 was concerned not with Lenin, but with Bogdanov, but everyone knew that he was on the edge of a precipice.

Creative philosophical thought cannot flourish in such an environment, and it amply accounts for the shuffling, the endless repetition, the monotony, the limitedness of Soviet philosophy, its petty sophistries, the reciprocal accusations and denunciations, the fundamental necessity of lying; neither talent nor genius can make any headway. The type of thought in process of elaboration is capable of an advanced degree of development, but its intellectual level could hardly be lower. It must be added, with sadness, that all this is a horrid caricature of Christianity. Christianity was the first system in history to appreciate all thought from the angle of orthodoxy or of heresy, that is, to give an example of communal thought. The authentic spirit of community, brotherhood (*sobornost*), is not collectivity, but too often in the course of history it has been supplanted by this collectivity which is so hostile to personality.

The most original and, in its way, the strongest characteristic of Marx-Leninist philosophy is the idea of an indissoluble union between theory and practice; for it, the unforgivable sin is a break between philosophy and politics, between speculation and social building-up. Purely speculative thought is therefore labelled bourgeois. Knowledge comes from action; abstract theorizing comes from the chasm which separates intellectual from physical work; that chasm must be filled up. This Marxist formula approximates to the central idea of N. F. Fedorov, for whom all evil sprang from the break between pure reason and practical reason and the consequent formation of a caste of "learned men"; he looked for the coming into the world of a knowledge that would transform and better it, that would be a "common work." This idea seems to me very Russian and very Christian. But Marx-Leninism has deprived it of its right nature and made it materialist, and therein, as in many other matters,

Communism is a caricature of the truth. For Communism, knowledge of nature is made real by the act of production, which is only to say again that knowledge is entirely subordinate to economic development as to the one only reality. It is the business of philosophy to be the power which directs revolutionary action and the organization of political warfare. Thus spake Lenin. The problem of Truth is a practical problem. Truth is revealed in deeds. From thence is drawn the conclusion that science and philosophy must be at the service of the Communist Party and cannot do anything else. Scientific impartiality is an impossibility, any attempt at objectiveness is indicative of bourgeois leanings. We shall see later on what difficulties this creates for the establishing of a criterion of truth. Marx-Leninists are bound to be ignorant of real philosophy, it just eludes them; only its most popularized forms are amenable to their critique. The reason lies in their mistaken notion of the "practical," that is, really, of life, of being, a notion which falsifies the scale of values, for in the end everything depends on how we order values. A "class-science" is nonsense, gnoseologically and logically. But it cannot be disputed that perversions of science can and do flourish; there is no such thing as "class-truth," but there is class error. There is some truth —not "class-truth," but plain truth—in certain Marxist considerations, but the Marx-Leninists evolve a sectarian conception of science which comes into collision with real objective science. In physics they even get to the stage where Lenin is put up against Einstein and Planck—which is really quite amusing.

The most noticeable thing is the importance accorded to the existence of a philosophical system. Politics are dependent on philosophic concepts. For example, the task is set to examine how the unorthodoxy of Trotsky is determined by his erroneous philosophy. Now Trotsky has never written anything about philosophy and has not got any. In the same way it is averred that the deviation towards "the right" of Bukharin, who was denounced as a partizan of the *kulaks*,* is due to his "mechanicist" materialism. Here Marx-Leninist materialism is clearly veering towards idealism, since it is deemed that consciousness determines being; it is difficult to suppose that Bukharin has *kulak* interests or Trotsky capitalist interests, therefore their deviation can have their origin only in a warped consciousness. We shall see, indeed, that the materialism of Russian communists often verges on idealism.

The Marx-Leninist idea of a "class-philosophy" denies in principle the existence of a universal human nature; it is a negation of the humanism founded on a recognition of the basis common to the whole of

* *Kulak*—one of the class of "wealthy" peasants as compared with "poor" or "middling" peasants.—Tr.

mankind, on the idea of universality. There is no possibility of discussion with Marx-Leninists; the arguer is relegated to the different type of consciousness of another "class" by the mere fact of daring to raise objections. Proletarian consciousness supposes the previous initiation into a mystery that is unseen and unintelligible from outside; "class-truth" is a sectarian truth which is made clear only to those who have made their way into the circle of initiates. There, a universalist line of argument has no meaning; facts themselves have no meaning, for they depend on consciousness, the proletarian consciousness, which with its philosophy and science, its morality and politics, calls for a definitive break with the past and its universalism and turns to the creation of a new world and a new man. Truth was revealed for the first time to this consciousness, revealed absolutely and finally; the Marxist revelation is as unique and complete as the Hegelian system was to its author. Progress is perfected; henceforward there can be no argument about its fundamental principles. It is an idea that leads to complete rationalization of the world, to a denial of all mystery, and it is a hatred of and opposition to mystery that provide the motive *pathos* of Marxism; mystery is only the result of anarchy in economic production, it is determined by a contingency. A close study of contemporary Soviet philosophy and anti-religious literature shows plainly that for the first time in the world's history an atheist sect has attained power, and it wields it over vast areas and huge numbers of people. The philosophy of this sect serves an end of a religious kind, its soul is anti-religious propaganda. This definition of Communism as an atheist sect must be distinguished from a judgement of it on its purely economic side. This socio-religious sect may have some truth and justice in it, but they are changed and perverted; and this change and perversion are the effect of the fixed idea which recognizes one sole value alone, disassociated from all other values and made into an absolute, which is equivalent to a transmutation of the relative into the absolute.

Two attitudes, two completely divergent positions, are possible for man, and he finds the face of everything different accordingly as he chooses the one or the other. He can if he will put himself in the presence of God and the mystery of being. Then he has a clear conscience and a clean heart, revelation and intuition are vouchsafed to him, the true primordial creative spirit appears, he reaches to the very source of all.

On the other hand, man can if he will put himself only in the presence of other men and with society. Then his conscience and his heart cannot be pure, revealed truth is changed, religion is reduced to a social fact, the light of intuition goes out and the glow of creation is cooled, and falsehood comes into its own, it is recognized as socially useful and even indispensable; man, whether conservative or revolutionary, is valued only in relation to the daily social routine and he can no longer attain to the ultimate source; even the voice of God can be heard only as an echo from the reality of society. This is not to say that man is not called to live in society and that he ought not to live socially, but that his social relations should be governed by a spirit turned towards the source of Being, and not *vice versa.*

Very well. Then it must be clearly stated that the Marx-Leninist never puts himself in the presence of God and the mystery of being but always in the presence of others and of society, in practice the Central Committee of the Communist Party. That is why he knows no revelations and has no intuitions. His heart and consciousness are completely circumscribed by the social creature, by other men. His philosophical speculation ignores the irrational and cannot even formulate the problem it presents. This orientation exclusively towards man in society and estrangement from the First Cause produce charlatanism—which can be perfectly sincere and loyal in individuals—in more or less all parties, schools, and sects. It provides a psychological problem of very great interest. In the Marx-Leninist philosophy this charlatanism, honest and even capable of self-sacrifice, is carried to its perfection; it is become a sacred duty. But freedom can come only from submission to God and to the mystery of being.

II

The "general line" of Marx-Leninist philosophy which the "collective" of young Red philosophers is engaged in elaborating represents the true and authentic dialectical materialism: *dialectical*, not any other form of materialism. It is stimulated by a bitter contest with two divergences, mechanistic materialism (Bukharin and the scientists, Timiriazev and several others) and dialectical idealism (Deborin with his disciple Karev and others).

The representatives of the "general line" use the prescriptions laid down by Stalin for the offensive on the philosophical front. He decreed, in effect, that Deborin's philosophy was nothing else than a menshevist idealism. The "general line" has to reveal and hold the philosophy of collectivism, it must be entirely purged of all personal opinions and inclinations, for in it, the Communist Party thinks, the proletariat itself becomes conscious. Nevertheless, the worst danger is seen in the mechanistic materialism which is associated with the right-wing trend in the Party and the *kulak* ideology. This type of materialism is looked on as foreign to Marxism and scorned as being merely popular; it is an obstacle to anti-religious propaganda because it can give no satisfaction to those who abandon religion; and it is accused of a wrong conception of matter, which it debases and from which it takes away the inherent life and movement; mechanicism sees the cause of movement in shocks from without and tries to explain everything by the action of environment. It is not at all "activist"; in sociology it accords a determining importance to "productive forces," that is to say, to economic phenomena disassociated from living creatures, so reducing the activity of "productive relations," namely, the strife of classes; this leads to what Soviet terminology calls "self-derivation." By this must be understood the thesis that everything produces itself in consequence of an objective economic process independent of the class-war. In the light of this necessarily deterministic interpretation of Marxism the dictation of the proletariat and of the Communist Party becomes impossible and meaningless. Now Soviet philosophy is essentially "activist" and wants above all to justify this dictation and its possibility even in a country with a rural economy, with an out-of-date capitalism, small proletariat, and overwhelming predominance of the peasant class. Then there is the question of which is the determining influence: productive forces or productive relations, the mechanism of the objective process of economic production or the dialectic of the active class-war with its limitless revolutionary will? This question has acquired a capital importance; it sums up the opposition between a mechanically passive conception and a dialectically active conception of matter, of the source of being. The question is equally pertinent to anti-religious propaganda: will religious beliefs disappear by the way of "self-derivation" or as the result of an intensive war against them? The theory of reflexes is unfavourable to all "activism," trying to explain everything by passive reaction to environment, and that is why the "general line" opposes it and resolutely attacks Pavlov and Bekhterev. The reflex theorists do not admit any difference between man and the lower animals and deny the autonomous nature of the psyche—surely a strange matter of complaint in the mouth of Marx-Leninists who still call themselves materialists!

The following example may explain the meaning of this strong opposition to "mechanicism," with its theory of environment and self-derivation. There is a strike of coal-miners in England. The reflex theorists explain the outbreak of this strike by the reaction of the workers to the acts of the government, its failure by the operation of natural laws, the condition of its social environment. No, say the Marx-Leninists, the failure of this strike is due to the treachery and cowardice of the English socialists. A purely moral explanation. This example is very significant. The "general line" will not admit any explanation by a simple reference to natural laws, to the objective course that events take; the reason for everything must be looked for in man, in class activity, in revolutionary or counter-revolutionary operations. Strictly speaking there are no immutable natural laws, for they can all be overcome and invalidated by man's social activity. Hence their open dislike of all naturalism in sociology, for it involves the admission of passivity, the denial of activity to individuals, classes, social groups, and parties; mechanicism and naturalism are not able to justify activity in man—social man, of course (no other exists for the Marx-Leninists). Therefore the objectively scientific side of Marxism, which bourgeois professors are pleased to put to the fore and Peter Struve expounded so clearly, gives place to "class-mysticism," a mysticism of action exempt from all limits. Social man is not just an extension and development of the world of living creatures as the mechanicists and naturalists claim, he is infinitely more. Darwinism, which is held of obligation in biology, is expressly condemned in sociology.

The mechanicists are continually being reproached for not understanding quality; only the representatives of dialectic can do that. Dialectical materialism does not confound the psychical with the physical as mechanicism does; its formula is: Psychical phenomena are as the inner surface of physiological processes; the unity of psychical and physical does not entail their identity. But that is not materialism at all, it is a psycho-physical parallelism. We are faced with the invariable weakness of materialism; it is not able to define itself, and in its efforts to do so it generally slips into some heterogeneity which is not materialism at all. The fact of the matter is that nobody knows what pure materialism is, least of all the materialists themselves. The Marx-Leninists revolt against the gross version of Büchner and Moleschott, for whom the brain secretes thought as the liver does bile. This sort of materialism arose by force of the popularized science which denied philosophy and its autonomy. The Marx-Leninists want to be philosophers and they uphold the rights of philosophy against the mechanicists and the absolute primacy of the natural sciences. What then is the weakness and defect of mechanicism in their eyes?

The answer is that the mechanicists deny dialectic, they do not consider matter from the dialectical angle, their matter is inert, dead; they do not know its great mystery, autodynamism (spontaneous movement). Dialectic is a philosophy, not a science, and philosophy has its own definition of matter distinct from that given by physics. Mechanicism cannot recognize autodynamism in material nature, or it regards it as immutable and eternal—the view of the eighteenth-century French materialists. Mechanicism does not see the contradiction inherent in matter and the autodynamism that springs from it, and it is for precisely that reason that it is not dialectical. Bukharin, in fact, has no idea of dialectic and recognizes only an antagonism. Yet according to the mechanicist theory it is impossible to resolve internal antinomies without the aid of dialectic; that must also be an authentic philosophy of the active struggle. Mechanistic materialism is the heir of the bourgeois philosophy of the "Enlightenment," it dates from before the days of Hegel-Marxist dialectic, and that is why it leaves the "general line" of Soviet philosophy on one side, it lacks its object. Mechanicism in sociology belongs to naturalism and biologism, theories that are expressly condemned; everything is determined by harmony or disharmony with environment. But that leads to the hateful theory of "self-derivation." From the mechanicist point of view one cannot conceive the emergence of a new society, because that can be brought about only by vigorous class-warfare. Revolutions are made, they do not make themselves; they require human freedom for conflict and action, as well as natural necessity. That may be called a philosophy of "social titanism," and it does not fit in at all with naturalistic determinism. Marx-Leninists also protest against the reduction from the complex to the simple which they impute to bourgeois science. The danger envisaged in the mechanicist deviation is simply the substitution of the mechanical for the dialectical, mechanics becoming the fundamental science from which all derives, which means the denial of autodynamism and therefore of action and struggle. According to the mechanicists the classes are passive in relation to productive forces, to the objective and regular economic process, and therefore Bukharin was openly on the side of the *kulaks*. Trotsky admits hardly any possibility of communism in an isolated country and for him peasants are the enemy class to the revolution. All that is quite logical and coherent.

Mach's theory also is firmly rejected, but opposition to it is not regarded as particularly important because the Communist Party at the moment includes partizans neither of him nor of Avenarius with whose philosophy and Marxism Bogdanov and Lunatcharsky attempted a conciliation when they belonged to the bolshevist group in the Party. Bogdanov even elaborated a whole philosophical system, "empirio-monism," and tried to constitute a science of universal organization called "tectology." Lenin scented the danger of this heresy and took Bogdanov and Lunatcharsky to task violently in his book on "materialism and empiric-criticism"—the only work of a philosophical character that he ever wrote, feeble in thought but polemically most powerful. In it he convicted the philosophy of Mach and Avenarius of being bourgeois-reactionary and therefore incompatible with Marxism. Bogdanov stuck to his heresy none the less, wrote several books, developed his system, and loyally separated himself from bolshevism during the revolution; he is now dead and his ideas have no influence among communists. As for Lunatcharsky, he had not the courage to defend Avenarius and gave up writing on philosophical matters; he enjoys no authority among the young communist philosophers, who attack him warmly. Mach's theory (Avenarius is equally involved) was rejected for the sole reason that it was not materialist—materialism is an inviolable symbol, and you are bound to profess it even though your philosophical doctrine is not materialist. Mach taught a sensationalist idealism, according to which being resolves itself into sensations and complexes of sensations. But the world of sensations rises above the distinction of physical and psychical. For Bogdanov, organization of experience is everything, the cosmic process and social whole being only different degrees in its development. The "general line" necessarily opposes a philosophy of this kind, which is quite foreign to dialectic and tends to Positivism rather than to Hegel (the Marx-Leninists have an especial dislike for all kinds of positivism on account of its bourgeois origins). Bogdanov's organization of experience is not at all a philosophy of the struggle born of the impact of contradictories; his way of looking at the social process showed him to be a naturalist. It must be noticed that he and the disciples of Mach are accused of leaning at the same time towards idealism and mechanicism, a mechanicism in this case resulting from the application of mechanistic speculation to social phenomena. The Marx-Leninists will never admit that life is only sensation, the organization of the "thing lived"; no: it is combat, the doing of deeds that remake the world, active construction, and these suppose the objective reality of the material world which is the scene of this strife and accomplishment. A world floating in sensations which are ordered to the interior of the cosmic process is not a favourable condition for war. Bogdanov would begin by forming a proletarian consciousness and culture (to which he gave a very conspicuous place in his system) before the communist revolution was undertaken, and indeed he never accepted the fact of that revolution. This idea could only be, and was, condemned, for it conflicts with what I have called the social titanism of the Soviets.

A far more grave heresy than mechanicism is the deviation towards Hegelian idealism represented by Deborin, editor of the review *Under the Flag of Marxism* which was for several years the organ of Soviet philosophy. Deborin, with Karev and others, has founded a whole school of young philosopher-dialecticians, and there again the "general line" is threatened. Dialectic is good in itself, it is necessary, Soviet philosophy must be dialectical—but it must never become infected with idealism and cease to be materialist. It is right to reverence Hegel, for from Hegel came Marx, and Lenin himself reverenced him. But God keep us from any inclination towards his idealism and from subjecting Marxism to "restatement." It must be understood that Deborin always calls himself a materialist (otherwise he could not live), but it is thought that there can be detected in him and his young followers a tendency towards idealism which comes from their devotion to Hegelian dialectic; they have gone too far in their opposition to mechanistic materialism. What happens to every heresy has happened to Deborin's; the truth in it (the opposing of dialectic to mechanicism) has been exaggerated, causing a divergence in the wrong direction and a break in the harmony of the orthodox system. The good work of Deborin's followers against mechanicism is recognized, but they have gone too far and must be themselves opposed. They are accused of separating philosophy from politics and the class-war, their dialectic is too abstract and not in touch with social construction, they do not join in anti-religious propaganda because they are indifferent to that great cause. Their chief fault is the absence of discrimination between the dialectic of Hegel and that of Marx, the one idealist, the other materialist and revolutionary; their own is too formal and academic, they are more interested in logic than in the social struggle. Moreover, Deborin has had the temerity to deny that Lenin was a great and original philosopher, and over-rates the importance of Plekhanov. Now according to the teaching of the "general line" Lenin represents a new phase in Marxism and dialectical materialism, corresponding to the period of imperialism and proletarian revolutions, and in this phase it is necessary definitively to subdue metaphysical materialism as well as idealism. Deborin does not realize that and has stopped short at Plekhanov.

Deborin's group is a proof that any excessive familiarity with Hegelian dialectic, any attempt at independent thought, is ruinous for materialism, which is the most childish and elementary of all forms of philosophy. Those of the younger men who have begun to think truly philosophically have all started to revise their materialism, while keeping the sacred name. The higher powers have stopped them in time and suggested that they should change their minds. Deborin is at present convicted of menshevist idealism and has no part in philosophical direction. This type of dialectical philosophy, like mechanicism and the theory of Mach, fails by its indifference to social titanism, to superhuman activity; it is too quiet and peaceable. Why, it gives to consciousness the primacy over being and to logic the primacy over material phenomena! Seen close to, dialectical materialism is an absurd reconcilement of the irreconcilable; that is why both dialectic and materialism must inevitably disappear. But the "general line" sets out to be a middle term between the mechanicist heresy (disappearance of dialectic) on the one hand and the dialectical idealist heresy (disappearance of materialism) on the other; it is revolutionary dialectical materialism in the classical form that Lenin gave to it. He disclosed the truth, dialectic, that is in idealism, but exaggerated it. Orthodox Soviet philosophy must once again set itself to reconcile what is not reconcilable. It will have radically to modify our conception of matter if it is going to succeed.

III

Marx-Leninist philosophy recognizes only two fundamental philosophical positions, idealism and materialism, and their difference is determined according to their answer to the capital question of the relationship between being and consciousness.

Idealism asserts the primacy of consciousness over being; materialism, of being over consciousness. If you recognize that being determines consciousness you are, by that fact alone, a materialist. We can see at once the fictitiousness and superficiality of such a classification, which is quite unjustifiable from the point of view of the history of philosophic thought. On this showing St. Thomas Aquinas would have to be considered a materialist, for he certainly recognized the primacy of being and would never have conceded that consciousness determined being. I should be surprised were my own philosophy qualified as materialist, and yet I am firmly convinced that being determines consciousness, and not the reverse. The classification does not take into account that one can be neither idealist nor materialist without being half-and-half. Christian philosophy is neither; it is realist. Or again, the existential philosophy of Heidegger or of Jaspers cannot be brought under either of these heads. Marxists always use the term materialism as synonymous with realism, having decided in advance that no other reality exists besides material reality; in all innocence they take the material world to be the one and only objective reality. When they say that being determines consciousness they mean that it is determined by matter and by the *ensemble* of material phenomena; as for consciousness itself, it is only an accident or reflection of the material world. The realism of the "general line" is, of course, untutored, an elementary dogmatism that has not been tested by the criticism of knowledge. And the Marx-Leninist theory of knowledge could not be more *simplist* or less critical. Lenin accepted a double criterion of truth: agreement with the real and agreement with the proletarian consciousness. One is bewildered by the puerility and inadequacy of this way of deciding the crucial point of philosophy. Lenin speaks of "agreement with the real." What does he mean by that? His followers have not attempted even to ask themselves the question which has troubled philosophic thought ever since the days of antiquity; how is the *trans-sensus*, the leap by which thought, consciousness, passes to objective reality, made possible? Does not the operation of our understanding rationalize the irrational real? They never suppose that the real, the objective data, can be spiritual, that the being which determines consciousness is spiritual. But above all does this double criterion of truth postulate a pre-established harmony of a special kind between the subjective and the objective aspects of the real. Thus agreement with the real always comes back to agreement with the proletarian consciousness. Only "class-philosophy" and "proletarian-science" correspond to the real and are free from the illusions and errors of consciousness. This objective-subjective criterion of truth and knowledge is not a fruit of the understanding or a purely cognitive postulate; it is an object of faith, of messianic faith in the proletariat. This accord of the thought and knowledge of the proletariat with reality can only be a matter of belief and not of rational knowing. Moreover, it appears that this thinking and knowing proletariat is not the empirical one of fact, but an ideal proletariat, bearer of the "proletarian idea" first revealed to the world by Marx. It follows that the consciousness of the proletariat can coincide with reality only as a transcendental, not as an empirical, consciousness, and so the criterion of truth becomes entirely idealist. The Marx-Leninist theory of knowledge does not go very far and is contained in a few sentences. Nor could it be otherwise. Materialism cannot have a theory of knowledge, and its criterion of truth is but elementary, forestalling the advent of critical examination. No criterion of truth can be discovered, from a materialistic standpoint, either in the subject or in the object, for the material world cannot furnish any such criterion. It must be remembered that Marx-Leninists are mortal foes of scepticism, agnosticism, and positivism (all of which are "bourgeois"), and so it happens that thought and intelligence touching the material world are transferred to the depths of matter itself. Thus material reality determines consciousness and makes knowledge possible, because consciousness and virtual thought are in that reality. In short, this dialectical materialism completely reverses the conception of matter and makes of it a myth endowed with divine properties.

The point of departure of the ontology of dialectical materialism is a cheap dogmatism which is indistinguishable from mechanistic materialism. The material world exists; it exists independently of consciousness, without beginning or end in time and space; there is no being other than this world of matter. Sometimes the difference between substance and phenomenon is indicated, with the object of showing that dialectical materialism is not a phenomenalism pure and simple: matter is substance, not phenomenon. The series of propositions that follows is a mixture of Hegelian pan-logism and the crudest popular materialism. Causality and the notion of law exist of themselves within the material world; causality is found actually in things, in matter. Logical categories are the relations and threads which unite real things together; the "general" is included in the "particular." Knowledge is a true reflection of things; thought is a form of motion, the refraction in the social man of universal evolution. The earth was prior to man (this "argument" drawn from a cheap naturalism is ceaselessly brought up against Christianity and all religion). Matter is absolute, knowledge is absolute; every trace of agnosticism or phenomenalism is removed. Dialectical materialism is an absolute system, for the absolute exists and is plainly knowable. Relativism, which follows logically from a materialistic conception of history, is hateful to the "general line"; Mach's functional conception of causality, all relativist positivism, all scepticism, are bourgeois and reactionary, while the methodical doubt of Descartes may not even be mentioned. The world is matter in motion in space and time; absolute truth resting upon absolute reality. Matter is endowed with unusual properties; all the riches of being are bestowed on it, it becomes spiritualized, it takes on an interior life, it is thought, the *logos*, liberty. Sensation appertains to matter, and much more than sensation.

It can be seen at a glance that this system is not properly speaking materialism but hylo-zoism.

Matter in motion represents at the same time both the evolution of the world and the passage from a lower to a higher. The autodynamism of matter is the cause of evolution. This conception of evolution in dialectical materialism is particularly *naïf*, for the distinction of a higher and a lower rests on a precedent judgement of value and supposes a hierarchy of values. But the problem of values is not even referred to. The fundamental idea of Soviet philosophy, autodynamism, is so developed in the "general line" that it can be regarded as something new, an original addition to the old Marxism. This metaphysical notion is intended to explain and justify the whole of communist politics. Motion in the universe is always a product of inherent autodynamism, and not of a shock from outside as mechanicism teaches; there is an internal contradiction in the depths of matter which produces motion from within. Motion, that is, change, supposes being and not-being. All that is undoubtedly taken from Hegel. But Soviet philosophy goes so far as to admit the spontaneity of motion in matter, and that spontaneity is especially dear to it. It provides the metaphysical justification of the dictatorship of the proletariat and proves the possibility of Communism in a backward agricultural country; it is a guarantee against all possible deviations. Free-will would even seem to be quasi-inherent in matter, which recalls the latest ideas of certain contemporary physicists about "free-will" in atoms. All interpretation of Marxism as an absolute determinism, particularly as a social determinism, is firmly rejected; I will even go so far as to say that the "general line" has arrived at a special sort of indeterminism, a system indispensable to a philosophy of conflict and action. Marxism, following Hegel, has always taught that freedom is a recognition of necessity; Marx-Leninism retains this idea but at the same time defines liberty as the spontaneity of the motion of each material particle. Any explanation by environment is treated with contempt and called mechanicism; everything is determined from within, so that it begins to look like a spiritualistic system. Matter is endowed with all the properties of the Hegelian spirit, and that is why dialectic makes its appearance. Dialectic, internal contradiction, autodynamism, these are in the world because pan-logism is inherent in matter.

History is logical and its own ineluctable logic can be seen right down to the class-war. It will even be said that everything that is most precious in the past must be taken in the negative. The revolution is logically defined as a leap, a solution of continuity in the passage from quantitative to qualitative. But the radical and hostile denial of all the historical thought of the past is clearly enough in contradiction with dialectic; dialectical development supposes that the past has its part in the future, that there is thesis and antithesis in the synthesis.

Marx-Leninism, however, makes history begin with itself, an absolutely anti-dialectical proceeding. It is continually slipping from dialectic to popular materialism and from that even to the hated mechanicism, and it cannot help it, for dialectical materialism is in an untenable position where is bred a perpetual conflict between dialectic and materialism. All its affirmations have a general character. For example, it is conceded (no one knows why) that the soul is part of the supernatural world and that the rejection of the supernatural world signifies the denial of the soul. The idea of the soul is only a trick of the "exploiters," and modern religion is discovered to be full of primitive animism. Nevertheless, the property peculiar to the psychical is recognized. The attribution of bourgeois and reactionary characteristics to the theories of electrons, *quanta*, and relativity is quite especially stupid; it is equivalent to a denial of all scientific discoveries and contemporary physics and to a beginning of really reactionary opinions. For they reproach physicists with having finally reached a complete denial of matter, and confront them with the physics of Lenin and the proletariat. But, as Lenin and the proletariat have no physics and have made no discoveries in that domain, they have to return to the dead theories of the nineteenth century. It is said over and over again that physics ought to be dialectical, but it remains simply a verbal declaration. The philosophical and scientific theories of the West are sometimes treated very sensibly and even impartially in *Militant Atheism.* It printed a most intelligent article on Vaihinger's *Philosophie des Als Ob*,* but after an objective analysis the writer is dragged through the mire of the grossest abuse. Vaihinger's philosophy of functionalism was denounced as bourgeois philosophy in decay and altogether reactionary. But no attempt is made to demonstrate in what way his philosophy (whose importance they exaggerate) is bourgeois-reactionary. It is probably because it is sceptical, relativist, and casts doubt on the existence of that reality wherein man is called on to act. Action is determined by the perception of reality. All the past has been lived in a state of conscious or unconscious falsehood; realities were not known for what they are, so that nobody could act in concert with the real. A single sempiternal truth is opposed to all the ideas of the past, namely, the moral truth which condemns the exploitation and oppression of the people.

The whole of this conception really rests on the assumption that there is identity between the objective nature of truth and the class-subjectivism of the proletariat. If that is shown to be doubtful, everything collapses. Many people, and among them the Marxists, have seen in historical materialism not

* Translated into English with the title of *The Philosophy of As If*, London, 1924.—Tr.

a theory or a dogma but a method, and as such it is liable to revision and development. But the Marx-Leninists are insistent that it is a theory, a doctrine, a system of dogmas, as well as a method. And they must do this, for not otherwise can their philosophy take on a "theological" character and their teaching be a religious teaching.

It is to be noticed that the Marx-Leninists systematically corrupt and misuse the terminology of traditional philosophy. The example was set by Engels, who arbitrarily opposed dialectic, the dynamic conception of a universe of motion and development, to the metaphysical static conception. According to this view, the German idealists of the beginning of the nineteenth century ought to be called anti-metaphysicians, and the French materialists of the eighteenth century, metaphysicians. This is why the philosophers of the "general line" call Bukharin a metaphysician; in fact, he does not understand dialectic. Actually, dialectic belongs to metaphysics (the dialectic of Plato, of Hegel), although a non-dialectical metaphysic is equally possible (*e.g.*, St. Thomas Aquinas, Spinoza). It is not right to oppose idealism with materialism. Realism should be opposed to idealism, and spiritualism to materialism (the theory of Mach has so little of idealism that it may well be called unqualified sensationalism). The notion itself of idealism is complex. The idealism of Plato came to birth in the struggle with sensationalism and has an ontological character; that of Kant is quite different and to a certain extent in opposition to Plato's. Husserl's phenomenological objectivism approaches both Platonic idealism and mediaeval realism. The Marx-Leninists are blind to all these shades of meaning. It is a significant fact that all the currents of Western philosophical thought which they take notice of and criticize are secondary and already rather antiquated. Kantian idealism, Avenarius, Mach, Vaihinger, Positivism, these are the systems which seem to them significant for to-day, and influential and widespread in "bourgeois civilization." The philosophical currents which are really characteristic of our time and of interest at present are the phenomenology of Husserl, Max Scheler and Heidegger, Jaspers, the metaphysical realism of N. Hartmann, Kroner's return to Hegelism, Thomism in France, dialectical theology in Germany, the idealist panmathematicism of Brunschwicg, the *Existenz Philosophie* of Soren Kierkegaard. All these are beyond the horizon of Soviet philosophers; they know simply nothing about them. The Marx-Leninists are all behind in their apologetics, just as Orthodoxy is. They have not got the least notion of the problem of the irrational, which is the fundamental problem of modern philosophy. The irrational systems are not contemplated by dialectical materialists because they are ignorant of them; in general, nothing problematical exists so far as they are concerned. Soviet philosophy has the mouldy smell of "provincial" thought. Although the word "materialism" retains the value of a sacred symbol, the term has ceased to designate any definite system. A philosophy of conflict and action has got to be created; the proletarian revolution and the proletarian dictatorship which it produced must absolutely be justified philosophically, independently of the influence of the exterior factors of evolution and without bringing in the quantitative element, the proletariat; their possibility must be securely founded on the qualitative element, the revolutionary class. An essential change in Marxism can be easily seen here; Leninism is already more than Marxism. It is a philosophy of quality and not of quantity, a special form of idealism, and a very emphasized idealism. The very reality with which Russian communism has to do is in a measure "cerebral," idealist, phantasmal, which only shows the power of ideas, the force of human action, the transfiguring might of myths and illusions. The fact of the existence of communist Russia is in itself a refutation of materialism.

IV

The diffusion of militant atheism is one of the principal tasks of Soviet philosophy; it was indeed to a considerable degree with a view to its accomplishment that this philosophy was adopted. The mechanicists are rebuked because their opinions are not capable of taking the place of faith with those who have abandoned religion, their materialism being too crude and elementary; the followers of Deborin, on the other hand, are accused of not being interested in anti-religious propaganda at all. In conformity with article 13 of the constitution of the Communist Party, every communist is bound to be atheist and to promote atheism; Communism cannot be Christian and in a general way cannot have a religion. In this connection an important incident happened concerning the Swedish communist Hedslund. He tried to maintain that a communist could be a believing Christian, that it was his own personal concern; and he was hotly opposed and abused by Yaroslavsky. It was henceforth held that religious opinions are not a private matter, as the liberal-democrats claim, but emphatically a social matter (the fact that they looked on religion as a personal concern was one of the reasons why the social-democrats were accused of treachery). Lenin solidly established the principle that religion is a personal matter in a bourgeois State and in such states the separation of Church and State should be required; but within the Communist Party it is not a personal matter but a concern of the Party. Once he is enrolled in it, the communist is committed to militant atheism. This requirement is a little modified in favour of industrial-workers and peasants who are admitted to the Party and accept its programme before they have quite got rid of all their superstitions and religious prejudices.

An express distinction is made between the anti-religious war of the philosophical experts and that of the revolutionary proletariat, a distinction made evident by the attitude taken up in dealing with Plekhanov. His views on religion are criticized in a special article in *Militant Atheism.* He is the founder of Marxism and of social-democracy in Russia, and in his time has exercised great influence in international social-democracy; but he has lost all authority among the young Marx-Leninists and is denounced as a traitor, menshevist, and adherent of the Fourth International. I think the Marx-Leninists are right, up to a point, when they label him an exponent of the philosophy of enlightenment, an "enlightener" of the people. He is of exactly that type and the materialistic principles of the eighteenth century "Enlightenment" are again incarnate in him. Our young Marx-Leninists think that he does not take religion seriously enough. His warfare against it is intellectual and scientific; he still thinks that religious beliefs will perish of themselves when the people have been sufficiently instructed and educated; hence the accusation that he ignores the "class" aspect of religion and the need for a "religious class-war." These philosophers fight religion with the weapons of bourgeois "free-thought," but Marx-Leninism is not free-thought and is contemptuous of the bourgeois free-thinker; philosophico-scientific criticism of religion is simply one department of the class-warfare with the exploiters. Plekhanov has not understood the part played by religion in exploitation. The "general line" philosophers reject all scientific theories about the origin of religion and of Christianity and dismiss all definitions of religion as bourgeois, and those Marxists such as Kunov, Plekhanov, and Kautsky who make use of them are warmly opposed. Kunov used to be looked on as a great authority, and his work *The Beginning of Religion and of Belief in God,* was published by the State publishing-house (*Gosisdat*) and recommended for use in propaganda. Now he is repudiated and violently criticized and the use of his book forbidden; he is not a dialectical materialist but a positivist, a follower of Tailor and other bourgeois authorities on animism; he misunderstood the social and "class" character that religion has always had. The Marx-Leninists will have nothing to do with any of the "bourgeois" scientific theories about religious belief: animism, naturalism, totemism, the mythological school's explanation of Christianity (denial of Christ's historical existence is obligatory), Freudian psychoanalysis as applied to religion. The only difficulty is that both Marx and Engels inclined to the naturalist view of the origin of belief. The Marx-Leninists take up an absolutely anti-historical standpoint and carry their warfare into the whole of past history; according to them religion has always and everywhere produced social oppression and exploitation, and the least allusion to any positive part it has played in the most distant past at once provokes angry animosity. The attacks on Christianity always have in view only its most popular (in the bad sense) and rudimentary forms and those which Christians themselves admit to be obscurantist and superstitious; the glories of Christianity, its saints and ascetics, its great thinkers, are deliberately ignored.

It must be allowed that this propaganda is often directed against the real shortcomings of Christians which we ourselves are forced to acknowledge, but it never touches Christianity itself. It is certainly painful to have to concede that the charges made against historical Christianity in an article by Yaroslavsky are three-quarters well founded and that we must take the blame. But on the other hand there is never a word about the high spiritual achievements of religious life; uninstructed readers of this propaganda are bound to receive the impression that no men of culture and intellectual attainments, endowed with a true creative genius, have ever been religious believers.

Soviet militant atheism is directed against all religions and every faith, but its sharpest point is turned towards Christianity. The fate of Kautsky's book *On the Origin of Christianity*, once regarded as the source-work on the subject, is typical. It was republished during the Soviet period with an introduction by Riazanov and was used officially in anti-religious propaganda, but now that is strictly forbidden; it is remembered that Kautsky has been a socialist traitor, a menshevist, an opponent of Bolshevism, and all his errors, wrongdoings, and treachery are attributed to his mistaken non-Marxist historical views. Marx-Leninists do not admit that bad practice is compatible with true theory; it is all one to them. Kautsky saw in primitive Christianity an effect of proletarian movements within the Roman empire; he saw Christ (the question of whose existence he thought of no importance) as a rebel and a revolutionary; and was not far from detecting a communistic character in his early followers in spite of the strong contrast between their community of goods and the Communism of to-day. *Militant Atheism* considered Kautsky's book in a special article, very well written. It is absolutely forbidden to attribute a proletarian and communist character to primitive Christianity; the argument may not be used in anti-religious propaganda because of the risk of thereby raising the prestige of Christianity in the eyes of the people and encouraging sympathy for it. The unfortunate Kautsky's opinion, although he concerned himself solely with economic phenomena, is declared to be "theological"—which is simply comic. Moreover, he explained the birth of Christianity by reference to its historical environment and its adaptation thereto, and this is denounced as mechanistic. The Christian phenomenon must be explained by the internal dialectic of social classes, by the struggle of men among themselves, by their autodynamism. Christianity, like every other religion, has been a social evil from the beginning and they even go so far as to assert that there were human sacrifices and sexual promiscuity in early Christian worship; that there were never any persecutions by the Roman emperors, they are a deliberate fable. And some of the phrases that are met with are of an absurdity passing all belief; for example, it is written that: "Behind the figures of the Buddha and of Christ the shameless face of Capitalism can be seen looming up." The weakness and failures within Christianity throughout the course of history lend colour to monstrous statements of this sort. Everything that has scientific pretensions in Soviet literature on religion is on an infinitely lower level than the philosophy of the "general line" which, after all, represents a certain effort of the mind; but when it is a question of religion, party passion and animosity paralyse thought altogether. Nevertheless, every means of playing on the emotions of the people is used with much skill, and many of the "stunts" are psychologically very clever. What are the fundamental themes and the weak spots at which they direct their blows?

Lenin's explanation of religion called for by the

necessities of the war of militant atheism is the only one accepted as scientific and as in conformity with the spirit of Soviet philosophy of the "general line." According to him, religion is an instrument of exploitation, a spiritual poison; it is a class phenomenon. Religion has always been the tool of exploitation and oppression, it has never had any positive value, never led, never helped, never contributed to the bettering of life; it has never defended the oppressed, it has always upheld the existing state of things and been a pillar of social immobility. Anti-religious literature dishes up the arguments of Feuerbach and Marx, but in a coarser form. Anticipation of the joys of Heaven distracts us from trying to improve our life on earth; religion offers an imaginary bliss, whilst it reflects man's real misery; Christian symbolism is only an expression of social relations with inequality, the domination of some over others, oppression. But the fundamental argument is that *religion in general, and Christianity in particular, is the negation of human activity.* Activity is the part of God, man is passive and listless; Christianity teaches that injustice and inequality should be patiently borne on earth and righteousness and happiness looked for in Heaven. Soviet philosophy holds so tightly to materialism because it is the radical negation of all transcendence and other-worldliness, which communists hate more than anything else; they see their worst enemy in faith in a transcendental world, in the existence of a transcendental being. The argument which is the most often used and considered to be the most convincing springs from this standpoint: the argument that believing Christians look to miracles and to divine grace for the betterment of their life; they celebrate offices to ask for a good harvest or for rain instead of improving agricultural technique and using tractors (technique is regarded as the best weapon against religion), and this does not accord with human activity. The methods of anti-religious propaganda are prepared particularly for a peasant environment, with an eye to forms of Christianity that are near enough to superstition and which do in fact discourage man's activity. Throughout history Christianity has often been used for that purpose, but that has nothing at all to do with the essence of it as the religion of the God-Man. Christianity does *not* teach that the Christian ought to expect a miracle always and in all matters, that man must not act, but leave it to God. For all that, the argument from human passivity still remains the strongest of all in the propagandist's armoury; it raises in the Christian conscience the problem of interpretation and of the justification of human activity. Marx-Leninists believe that the rationalization of political economy means the end of mysticism and religion, there will be no room left for mystery; it is the anarchy of capitalist production that breeds religious beliefs. This is a very frail argument which corresponds not at all with reality, for it is precisely during the capitalist epoch that religion has been weakened and it is the contradictions of Capitalism that drive men to atheism. Marx-Leninists believe that a controlled economy that makes the life of men depend on organized activity, a rationalization of every side of life, must by doing away with chance at the same time do away with religion and usher in the triumph of materialism. But there is no need to wait for these things to happen by themselves by the force of autodynamism; they must be forwarded by the anti-religious war. Its propaganda is a sacred duty and philosophy must be at its service; this task on the philosophical front is an integral part of the Five-Year Plan. Moreover, a distinction is made between anti-religious propaganda and the persecution of religion, a discrimination on which the propagandists insist very strongly. In their textbooks and discussions of method there is a continual disparagement of the forced closing of churches and of sacrilege. "Don't make martyrs!" is the cry of Yaroslavsky and his henchmen. It doesn't pay; it leads to religious reaction and a strengthening of faith among the people. They review all the examples of where wrongs have been done, zeal carried too far, open persecution engaged in, and recommend abstention from such methods as deviations and deformations of their proper work. We know that in practice they do make martyrs, that almost every priest is put in the position of a martyr, but these things are not interpreted as religious persecution, they are political measures against counter-revolutionaries. As for the feast-days, they are said to have the reactionary effect of mollifying the hate of the workers for the exploiters.

It is curious to notice that the members of non-conformist sects are looked on as more dangerous than the Orthodox believers. Orthodoxy appears to them as the lowest, most passive, most superstitious, and most obscurantist form of Christianity, and it is easily overcome. The religion of the sects (it is probably principally the Baptists that they have in view) is an improved form of Christianity, less reactionary from the social standpoint. The sectaries are far more active than the Orthodox, they show more skill in meeting the offensive, and therefore they are a more dangerous enemy. They may even be communists, but then they repudiate class-war by violence and enfeeble the activities of the workers. Their ministers, "priests-in-trousers," are deemed more dangerous than "priests-in-cassocks"; they are an elusive enemy, more cultured and better armed. Priests-in-cassocks are allowed still to exist, though under grinding conditions and with a very narrow curtailment of their religious activities, thanks to opportunist concessions granted to the remains of superstition among the people; but priests-in-trousers are absolutely refused the right to live in

Soviet territory. God may be spoken of in church during service-time, but apart from that no one is permitted to refer to him. Strictly speaking all non-materialists, non-Marxists, free philosophers, all men with spiritual desires, belong to the category of priests-in-trousers; it is a prodigiously large category, every idealist or spiritualist philosopher belongs to it. Einstein is a priest-in-trousers. Even Lunatcharsky is suspect. The ideas of the priests-in-trousers are more troublesome than those of the priests-in-cassocks because they cannot be fought with too elementary arguments; above all do the Marx-Leninists hate the truly spiritual forms of religious life and thought. Lenin declared roundly that a Catholic *abbé* who corrupts young girls is preferable to a chaste good-living priest, because he is so much easier to deal with. Nothing is more disliked by Marx-Leninists than attempts at conciliation between Christianity and communistic Socialism. They dread that the Church might adapt herself to Socialism in order to gain the souls of the workers. They believe that her hostility to Communism is determined not only empirically by the facts, but follows from her very doctrine. I am assured that a bourgeois full of capitalist greed is more tolerable, more acceptable as a fellow-traveller, to a militant atheist than is a Christian communist. As for the anti-religious propaganda itself, it is a complex mixture. There is indubitably an educative element for the instruction of the unlettered people, but it is closely bound up with atheism and a new and frightful idolatry.

V

To sum up our analysis: The attitude of the Marx-Leninists towards philosophy and religion is determined in the first place by the requirements of an active warfare, and accordingly Soviet philosophy may at first sight give an impression of pragmatism. But it in fact condemns pragmatism and proclaims the existence of an objective absolute Truth which corresponds to reality. The power and fulness of the faith of the Marx-Leninists, their incapacity for doubt and for critical reflection, are astounding. Their search for a synthetic philosophical system, wherein theory and practice shall be indissolubly unified, is admirable in many respects: we must do the same—but in quite another name. They wish to produce a new man, a new psychical entity, and it is possible that they will succeed better in that than in building a new economy. Psychologically they have done much—and it is very frightening. Their communistic economy is much more neutral and much less intimidating. We, too, must put our hopes in the birth of a new man, in the creation of a new psychical entity, but one grounded on the eternal truth of Christianity. The Marx-Leninists have drawn up an imposing plan for a radical reconstruction of social life: that is their strength. But they are coming under the sway of a colourless impersonalism. They have thrown away all the old sacred things and age-long values and bow before a novel sacredness and new values, and these new things do not dwell in the heights of Being, but move among the slums; their passion for social justice alone belongs to a better world.

The Marx-Leninists do not see the prophetic side of religion and they have a dark "prophetism" of their own. Their notion of Christianity as an obscurantist faith for slaves considerably eases the task they have before them, and unhappily they meet a good many Christians who fit into such a description; as for their conception of the world, an often merely verbal materialism is not essential to it; they are not materialists at all, but profess a sort of lightless spiritualism. What is essential to them is atheism, hatred of Christianity. For all that it has a certain truth in it, Communism is the utter limit of social idolatry; it is consistent with itself and affirms the absolute supremacy of society over man, over individuals, over their souls. Communists stake their all on the outward social warfare and stifle all anxiety about the meaning of personal life and the destiny of a human being face to face with Eternity. Their philosophy, slave to the passing hour, never contemplates the problems of suffering and death, the meaning of that which was and is not, eternity.

Their simpleness is particularly shown by their not understanding that everything is ultimately determined by a fundamental and ageless hierarchy of values. The problem of values simply does not exist for them, in spite of all their speculation and all their action being dominated by the fact that they have exalted social, economic, and technical values as sovereign—a conception that in no way corresponds to the complexity and variety of the real which they pursue, which is entirely out of harmony with the mystery of Being. Their philosophy is not a philosophy of human existence, whatever their affirmations about the activity of class-man may be, but a philosophy of objects and things. For them, truth is only a weapon of war exuding hate; a truth appertaining not to Eternity, but to the Five-Year Plan. Their task is the equitable organization of human society, and it has been entrusted to them according to the mysterious disposition of divine providence; and by them the grandeur of that task has been brought low, defiled, dishonoured.

A BRIEF OVERVIEW OF NIKOLAI BERDYAEV'S LIFE AND WORKS

Nikolai Berdyaev (1874–1948) was one of the greatest religious thinkers of the 20th century. His adult life, led in Russia and in western European exile, spanned such cataclysmic events as the Great War, the rise of Bolshevism and the Russian Revolution, the upsurge of Nazism, and the Second World War. He produced profound commentaries on many of these events, and had many acute things to say about the role of Russia in the evolution of world history. There was sometimes almost no separation between him and these events: for example, he wrote the book on Dostoevsky while revolutionary gunfire was rattling outside his window.

Berdyaev's thought is primarily a religious metaphysics, influenced not only by philosophers like Kant, Hegel, Schopenhauer, Solovyov, and Nietzsche, but also by religious thinkers and mystics such as Meister Eckhart, Angelus Silesius, Franz van Baader, Jakob Boehme, and Dostoevsky. The most fundamental concept of this metaphysics is that of the *Ungrund* (a term taken from Boehme), which is the pure potentiality of being, the negative ground essential for the realization of the novel, creative aspects of existence. A crucial element of Berdyaev's thought is his philosophical anthropology: A human being is originally an "ego" out which a "person" must develop. Only when an ego freely acts to realize its own concrete essence, rather than abstract or arbitrary goals, does it become a person. A society that furthers the goal of the development of egos into persons is a true community, and the relation then existing among its members is a sobornost.

He showed an interest in philosophy early on, at the age of fourteen reading the works of Kant, Hegel, and Schopenhauer.

While a student at St. Vladimir's University in Kiev, he began to participate in the revolutionary Social-Democratic movement and to study Marxism. In 1898, he was sentenced to one month in a Kiev prison for his participation in an anti-government student demonstration, and was later exiled for two years (1901–02) to Vologda, in the north of Russia.

His first book, *Subjectivism and Individualism in Social Philosophy* (1901), represented the climax of his infatuation with Marxism as a methodology of social analysis, which he attempted to combine with a neo-Kantian ethics. However, as early as 1903, he took the path from "Marxism to idealism," which had already been followed by such former Marxists as Peter Struve, Sergey Bulgakov, and S.L. Frank. In 1904 Berdyaev became a contributor to the philosophical magazine *New Path*. The same year he married Lydia Trushcheva, a daughter of a Petersburg lawyer. In 1905–06, together with Sergey Bulgakov, he edited the magazine *Questions of Life*, attempting to make it the central organ of new tendencies in the domains of socio-political philosophy, religious philosophy, and art. The influence exerted upon him by the writers and philosophers Dmitry Merezhkovsy and Zinaida Gippius, during meetings with them in Paris in the winter of 1907–08, led him to embrace the Russian Orthodox faith. After his return to Russia, he joined the circle of Moscow Orthodox philosophers united around the Path publishing house (notably Bulgakov and Pavel Florensky) and took an active part in organizing the religious-philosophical Association in Memory of V. Solovyov. An important event in his life at this time was the publication of his article "Philosophical Truth and the Truth of the Intelligentsia" in the famous and controversial collection *Landmarks* (1909), which subjected to a critical examination the foundations of the world-outlook of the left-wing Russian intelligentsia. Around this time, Berdyaev published a work which inaugurated his life-long exploration of the concept of freedom in its many varieties and ramifications. In *The Philosophy of Freedom* (1911), a critique of the "pan-gnoseologism" of recent German and Russian philosophy led Berdyaev to a search for an authentically Christian ontology. The end result of this search was a philosophy of freedom, according to which human beings are rooted in a sobornost of being and thus possess true knowledge.

In 1916, Berdyaev published the most important work of his early period: *The Meaning of the Creative Act*. The originality of this work is rooted in the rejection of theodicy as a traditional problem of the Christian consciousness, as well as in a refusal to accept the view that creation and revelation have come to an end and are complete. The central element of the "meaning of the creative act" is the idea that man reveals his true essence in the course of a continuing creation realized jointly with God (a theurgy). Berdyaev's notion of "theurgy" (in contrast to those of Solovyov and Nikolai Fyodorov) is distinguished by the inclusion of the element of freedom: the creative act is a means for the positive self-definition of freedom not as the choice and self-definition of persons in the world but as a "foundationless foundation of being" over which God the creator has no power.

Berdyaev's work from 1914 to 1924 can be viewed as being largely influenced by his inner experience of the Great War and the Russian Revolution. His main themes during this period are the "cosmic collapse of humanity" and the effort to preserve the hierarchical order of being (what he called "hierarchical personalism"). Revolutionary violence and nihilism were seen to be directly opposed to the creatively spiritual transformation of "this world" into a divine "cosmos." In opposing the chaotic nihilism of the first year of the Revolution, Berdyaev looked for support in the holy ontology of the world, i.e., in the divine cosmic order. The principle of hierarchical inequality, which is rooted in this ontology, allowed him to nullify the main argument of the leveling ideology and praxis of Communism—the demand for "social justice." Berdyaev expressed this view in his *Philosophy of Inequality* (1923).

During this period, Berdyaev posed the theme of Russian messianism in all its acuteness. Torn apart by the extremes of apocalyptic yearning and nihilism, Russia is placed into the world as the "node of universal history" (the "East-West"), in which are focused all the world's problems and the possibility of their resolution, in the eschatological sense. In the fall of the monarchy in February 1917, Berdyaev saw an opportunity to throw off the provincial Russian empire which had nothing in common with Russia's messianic mission. But the Russian people betrayed the "Russian idea" by embracing the falsehood of Bolshevism in the October Revolution. The Russian messianic idea nevertheless remains true in its ontological core despite this betrayal.

In the fall of 1919, Berdyaev organized in Moscow the Free Academy of Spiritual Culture, where he led a seminar on Dostoevsky and conducted courses on the Philosophy of Religion and the Philosophy of History. This latter course became the basis of one of his most important works: *The Meaning of History: An Essay on the Philosophy of Human Destiny* (1923). His attacks against the Bolshevik regime became increasingly intense: he called the Bolsheviks nihilists and annihilators of all spiritual values and culture in Russia. His activities and statements, which made him a notable figure in post-revolutionary Moscow, began to attract the attention of the Soviet authorities. In 1920, he was arrested in connection with the so-called "tactical center" affair, but was freed without any consequences. In 1922, he was arrested again, but this time he was expelled from Russia on the so-called "philosopher's ship" with other ideological opponents of the regime such as Bulgakov, Frank, and Struve.

Having ended up in Berlin, Berdyaev gradually entered the sphere of post-War European philosophy; he met Spengler, von Keyserling, and Scheler. His book *The New Middle Ages: Reflections on the Destiny of Russia and Europe* (1924) (English title: *The End of Our Time*) brought him European celebrity. Asserting that modern history has come to an end, and that it has been a failure, Berdyaev again claimed that Russia (now the post-revolutionary one) had a messianic mission. He wrote that "culture is now not just European; it is becoming universal. Russia, which had stood at the center of East and West, is now—even if by a terrible and catastrophic path—acquiring an increasingly palpable world significance, coming to occupy the center of the world's attention" (*The New Middle Ages*, p. 36). In 1924, Berdyaev moved to Paris, where he became a founder and professor of the Russian Religious-Philosophical Academy. In 1925, he helped to found and became the editor of the Russian religious-philosophical journal *Put'* (*The Path*), arguably the most important Russian religious journal ever published. He organized interconfessional meetings of representatives of Catholic, Protestant, and Orthodox religious-philosophical thought, with the participation of such figures as Maritain, Mounier, Marcel, and Barth.

In the émigré period, his thought was primarily directed toward what can be called a liberation from ontologism. Emigration became for him an existential experience of "rootless" extra-hierarchical existence, which can find a foundation solely in "the kingdom of the Spirit," i.e., in the person or personality. The primacy of "freedom" over "being" became the determining principle of his philosophy, a principle which found profound expression in his book *On the Destiny of Man: An Essay on Paradoxical Ethics* (1931), which he considered his "most perfect" book. This is how he expressed this principle: "creativeness is possible only if one admits freedom that is not determined by being, that is not derivable from being. Freedom is rooted not in being but in 'nothingness'; freedom is foundationless, is not determined by anything, is found outside of causal relations, to which being is subject and without which being cannot be understood" (from his autobiography, the Russian version, *Self-knowledge*, p. 231).

At around the same time, Berdyaev re-evaluated Kant's philosophy, arriving at the conclusion that only this philosophy "contains the foundations of a true metaphysics." In particular, Kant's "recognition that there is a deeper reality hidden behind the world of phenomena" helped Berdyaev formulate a key principle of his personalism: the doctrine of "objectification," which he first systematically developed in *The World of Objects: An Essay on the Philosophy of Solitude and Social Intercourse* (1934) (English title: *Solitude and Society*). This is how Berdyaev explained this doctrine: "Objectification is an epistemological interpretation of the fallenness of the world, of the state of enslavement, necessity, and disunitedness in which the world finds itself. The objectified world is subject to rational knowledge in concepts, but the objectification itself has an irrational source" (*Self-knowledge*, p. 292). Using man's creative powers, it is possible to pierce this layer of objectification, and to see the deeper reality. Man's "ego" (which knows only the objectified world) then regains its status of "person," which lives in the non-objectified, or real, world. Berdyaev had a strong sense of the unreality of the world around him, of his belonging to another—real—world.

After the Second World War, Berdyaev's reflections turned again to the role of Russia in the world. His first post-war book was *The Russian Idea: The Fundamental Problems of Russian Thought of the 19th Century and the Beginning of the 20th Century* (1946), in which he tried to discover the profound meaning of Russian thought and culture. Himself being one of the greatest representatives of this thought and culture, he saw that the meaning of his own activity was to reveal to the western world the distinctive elements of Russian philosophy, such as its existential nature, its eschatalogism, its religious anarchism, and its obsession with the idea of "Divine humanity."

Berdyaev is one of the greatest religious existentialists. His philosophy goes beyond mere thinking, mere rational conceptualization, and tries to attain authentic life itself: the profound layers of existence that touch upon God's world. He directed all of his efforts, philosophical as well as in his personal and public life, at replacing the kingdom of this world with the kingdom of God. According to him, we can all attempt to do this by tapping the divine creative powers which constitute our true nature. Our mission is to be collaborators with God in His continuing creation of the world.

Summing up his thought in one sentence, this is what Berdyaev said about himself: "Man, personality, freedom, creativeness, the eschatological-messianic resolution of the dualism of two worlds—these are my basic themes."

BORIS JAKIM
2009

E

BIBLIOGRAPHY OF NIKOLAI BERDYAEV'S BOOKS IN ENGLISH TRANSLATION

(IN ALPHABETICAL ORDER)

The Beginning and the End. Russian edition 1947. First English edition 1952.

The Bourgeois Mind and Other Essays. English edition 1934.

Christian Existentialism. A Berdyaev Anthology. 1965.

Christianity and Anti-Semitism. Russian edition 1938. First English edition 1952.

Christianity and Class War. Russian edition 1931. First English edition 1933.

The Destiny of Man. Russian edition 1931. First English edition 1937.

The Divine and the Human. Russian edition 1952. First English edition 1947.

Dostoevsky: An Interpretation. Russian edition 1923. First English edition 1934.

Dream and Reality: An Essay in Autobiography. Russian edition 1949. First English edition 1950.

The End of Our Time. Russian edition 1924. First English edition 1933.

The Fate of Man in the Modern World. First Russian edition 1934. English edition 1935.

Freedom and the Spirit. Russian edition 1927. First English edition 1935.

Leontiev. Russian edition 1926. First English edition 1940.

The Meaning of History. Russian edition 1923. First English edition 1936.

The Meaning of the Creative Act. Russian edition 1916. First English edition 1955.

The Origin of Russian Communism. Russian edition 1937. First English edition 1937.

The Realm of Spirit and the Realm of Caesar. Russian edition 1949. First English edition 1952.

The Russian Idea. Russian edition 1946. First English edition 1947.

Slavery and Freedom. Russian edition 1939. First English edition 1939.

Solitude and Society. Russian edition 1934. First English edition 1938.

Spirit and Reality. Russian edition 1946. First English edition 1937.

Towards a New Epoch. Transl. from the original French edition 1949.

Truth and Revelation. English edition 1954.